D0350198

*

Finding Our Father

*

231.6
Al53f

FINDING
OUR
FATHER

*

Diogenes Allen

*

JOHN KNOX PRESS
Atlanta, Georgia

9611

HIEBERT LIBRARY
PACIFIC WITHDRAWN MINARY
FRESNO, CALIF. 93702

Unless otherwise noted, Scripture quotations are from the *Revised Standard Version of the Bible*, copyrighted 1946 and 1952.

Library of Congress Cataloging in Publication Data

Allen, Diogenes.
  Finding our father.

  Includes bibliographical references.
  1. God.   2. Love   3. Death   4. Jesus
Christ—Resurrection. I. Title.
BT102.A43   231'.6   73–16917
ISBN 0–8042–0557–4

© John Knox Press 1974
Printed in the United States of America

ACKNOWLEDGMENTS

*

Johan Christiaan Beker, Professor of Biblical Theology, Princeton Theological Seminary, the Reverend Raymond I. Lindquist, Jr., Pavilion, New York, and my wife Jane Mary all deserve my gratitude for the many ways they have helped me, above all for talking over my ideas with me as they were developing.

CONTENTS

*

*

Finding Our Father

*

Chapter One

THE PANIC IN THEOLOGY

*

The claims now made in theology are much more modest than those formerly put forward. There has been a loss of confidence. Yet our life still baffles us and demands to be understood. Consider, for example, the experience of a young doctor. She was feeling rather sorry for herself as she made the rounds of the children's ward, having left behind her own children and husband to celebrate Christmas without her. One little boy could hardly wait for her to get to him. He had a present for her which he had badgered his mother for days to buy. Naturally the doctor was pleased to receive the gift, but she did not think too much about it as she went about her work that day. That evening the child died.

This incident is indeed a terrible one, a part of the common reality that meets us all in one form or another. But what is the point of relating it? It tends to bring tears to our eyes, and makes us think, How terrible! It might make a few of us silently vow to be more loving, more kindly, more humane. If it does have this more permanent effect, well and good. But in relating it, I wanted primarily to have us notice two things. First, how much love, how much gratitude and affection even a small boy of nine can feel. We tend to forget just how much love a human being can have. How can such love pass away? How can a creature that has so much to give simply disappear? Second, how we see things from our own point of view, most of the time. While this child was longing for his doctor to come, longing to give his present, this doctor was wrapped up inside herself, thinking about her bad luck in having to work on Christmas Day. Her feelings were perfectly natural, yet how far from being in contact with the feelings of this little boy. A great deal of our life is spent this way: seeing things from our own point of view, and thereby being out of contact, out of touch with great and radiant realities all around us. Why is it this way? How can we escape from this enclosure that is ourselves, that limits our horizon and keeps us from noticing others?

When I ask questions like these, I do not ask them as a psychologist nor as a philosopher but as one who believes in God. I want to know the relationship between God and the enormous affection that a person potentially can know; I want to learn how God can affect the personal point of view from which we see things most of the time.

All of us have ordinary experiences connected with such things as washing clothes, preparing meals, being interrupted by a child while reading a book, having to struggle to meet a deadline at work. These experiences are not different from the dramatic experience of a doctor working on Christmas Day. Our ordinary experiences are nearly all experiences in which things are seen from our own personal point of view, a point of view that closes us off from the deep affection that is within both ourselves and others. Our concern throughout this book is to open our eyes to the significance of our ordinary experiences, to see the abiding realities that are there for us to experience, by showing us how God is related to them.

To do this, however, requires us to think about God, and that has become difficult for many of us in recent years. We feel less confident in talking about God. There are many reasons for this, only one of which interests us here: the difficulty of finding room for God in our universe, a difficulty leading to a near-panic among theologians during the past ten years. For centuries people have been accustomed to explain the very existence of the universe and to account for its marvelous order by reference to God. Until late in the seventeenth century it was generally thought that all biological growth and decay, and all motion from one place to another, had their ultimate explanation in God. And for nearly a century after that, leading scientists thought God performed such jobs as replacing energy believed to have been lost in the collision of bodies. God, in short, was an integral part of philosophical and scientific theories well into the modern era.

But now the pattern has been reversed, and there seems to be nothing which we can legitimately use God to explain. Item after item once explained by reference to God is now explained without reference to him. Even more important has been the development of the idea of a self-contained universe. Every field of investigation seeks to solve its problems without any reference to God. A historian now would not think of listing as one of the causes of the French Revolution God's chastisement of the French people for their sins, as would some historians at that time. The social sciences do not use the concept of original sin because it is of no apparent use to them in their attempts to explain and control human behavior. We in fact do not know that the universe is self-contained, but we proceed on that basis in all the recognized university disciplines because such a procedure has been so successful with the problems treated in those disciplines.

Perhaps something of our plight can be captured by recalling the way we talk to children about God. Have not we all told a child on some occasion that God is everywhere? A child, of course, does not understand how this is possible, and usually tells us so. And since he cannot see God, it is almost as though he had been told that God is nowhere. But actually it is not only children but adults as well who have trouble understanding this truth. We usually can grasp only the negative, namely, that God is not limited to one place, as we are. But this does not help us to conceive of God, or to recognize his presence. What we need is to perceive his actual presence, to recognize his reality quite concretely in the midst of our world and its workings, and in the midst of our lives.

But it has become difficult to find God's presence precisely because of his lack of real connection with our needs and desires. In all religions there is the promise of aid or comfort, a promise of at least some degree of fulfillment, and often an escape from the threat of terrible dangers to which one is liable. But these promises often do not touch our lives as profoundly or as deeply as we would like. Moreover, Freud has made us very conscious of the power of wishful thinking. We are suspicious of any view of reality which is in fundamental accord with how we would like things to be. We are suspicious of such beliefs as a life beyond death; a savior and protector to whom we pray with confidence; and a place of central importance for us in the universe. It is widely felt that we ought to be able to cope with the challenges to our corporate life without going outside the universe for aid. There is a widespread conviction that an individual should not need God to cope with reality. Religious belief is considered to be a crutch and a failure to come to full maturity.

But not only are their needs suspect, people's desires are also changing. Because of this shift in desires, the traditional views of God's ways of helping people seem to be remote from human experience. Consider, for example, what a Christian in, let us say, ninth-century Britain would look to God for. There was the ever present possibility of famine; illness and disease, including pathologies which happily now are utterly trivial, were common and dreaded, while most means of easing pain were ineffective; childbirth and child-rearing were hazardous; there was constant fear of attack by fierce Norsemen, whose way of life was robbery and plunder. There was the fear of dreadful spirits and terrifying powers. The gospel of a gracious God, whose Son was born of a humble maiden, who suffered at men's hands yet who had power over all nature, over demons, and over death itself, was indeed about a God who impinged deeply on their needs. Yet he did not merely comfort and sustain, he elevated their desires and aspirations. They were called upon to realize a society of justice, even of brotherhood, and their achievements in these respects are impressive.

Compare this to the world in which we live in the West. There is no need to fear God in the least, for we are assured by the clergy of his love. Why seek forgiveness from him, when he is not a judge or one who holds us responsible? We do not even need to ask to be forgiven. Few people believe in demons or evil spirits. For illness, most religious people go to doctors, and only when desperate perhaps, turn to faith healers; death is massively denied (as we will show later). If someone wants anything, then he had better see to it himself, for God is not really thought to be capable of doing anything about it. What is there to look to God for?

Our desires are powerfully this-worldly; that is, without a thought that the true life is to be found by contact with God, and with those who are in contact with him. This is most evident in those attempts to connect God to the "with it" values of the moment. "Openness" and "freedom" are big; no mention is made of Kierkegaard's claim that Christianity has to do with forsaking the world, or Saint Francis' Lady Poverty (some touches among the fringe youth, but hardly aspired to by the clergy or laity); not a whisper about the overwhelming power of envy which well-nigh rules us. This is not the stuff that brings one to one's knees, fills one's heart with warmth, kindles in one the aspiration to loving service, or fills one with self-forgetful adoration.

Perhaps the most sustained effort to relate God to our contemporary needs is in political theology. God has been associated with revolution and men's deliverance from all earthly evil—poverty, alienation, powerlessness. This theology has given some, whose grip on religion had become precarious, a new lease on life; and it has genuinely inspired some stalwarts to a new perception of the gospel. But because there is a fear that this world will be neglected for a pursuit of the next,[1] men's needs are conceived of in a limited way, and God who meets men's needs is accordingly pictured in a limited way. Moreover, revolutions, history, and political aspirations have not been satisfactorily explained by reference to God. The use of Scripture is often highly questionable, and the persuasiveness of viewing the universe as self-contained is untouched.

If concern for God, and for what he and only he can do for us, are powerfully at work in people, then theology becomes a vital and even a life-giving pursuit. Instead, much theology has become primarily directed to this-worldly concerns; and the solution of these concerns is taken as the basic rationale for a belief in God. The rest of our religious heritage is ignored. When only this-worldly concerns are considered fundamental, then only an attentuated picture of God, or a low-theology, is possible. But since it is very hard to reach Christianity's world view by hard-nosed argument, or to handle the truly massive shift in men's concerns, an attentuated Christianity has resulted.

To be overwhelmed by these difficulties is to fail to recognize that God is a *presence*, not just the conclusion of an argument or merely an entity in an intellectual construction. Because he is a presence, we can become aware of him or learn to recognize him. One way in which this recognition may take place, or be improved, is through the very portrayal of him and of a universe related to him. There is no need to wait until one has the support of the intellectual or social milieu of one's time *before* one begins to portray him and a universe under him. The latter may lead to the former.

The notion that God is a presence also very much affects the basis for belief. It means that it is necessary *to get oneself into a position* whereby one can recognize his presence. One cannot take it for granted that there is only one viewpoint from which to survey what there is and from which we recognize or are aware of such a presence. To live, move, and have one's being in God is to be able to move from one viewpoint to another, and back and forth, and be perhaps simultaneously aware of more than one viewpoint (e.g., it is but bread, but also the body of Christ, a first-century Jew and the eternal Son of God). In addition, it is not necessary to recognize God all at once or in his fullness, but he can be recognized gradually as layer after layer of understanding is attained. It involves learning to move from a viewpoint in which our self-concern and our power distort our vision.

This perception of the presence of God can be illustrated by a description of an experience as found in the novel *The Unicorn* by Iris Murdoch. I use the experience of perfect love she attributes to one of her characters to explain what I mean by the expression "getting into a position" and in particular getting into a position to have the experience she describes. We will see why this experience is so extraordinarily difficult to attain and to sustain. This experience not only allows us to illustrate the nature of perfect love but also to give an account of what people are.

The next step will be to provide a framework for this experience: this framework is composed of familiar Christian beliefs; in particular, the doctrines of creation, the Trinity, and the kingdom of God. This is done partly to show how an emotional experience or a perception can be the bearer of truth. Consider, for example, the remark made about Martin Buber to the effect that a person who has never had the I-Thou experience Buber talks about has no heart, but as far as philosophy is concerned, there is no more to be said about it.[2] Buber himself considered it to be of supreme importance, as the orienting truth of the universe. But one can acknowledge the existence of the experience and not consider it the fundamental truth about the universe.

The framework of Christianity elevates the experience Murdoch describes to a place of supreme importance and explains how an emotional experience can be the bearer of truth. In addition, this perception, which is said to be one of perfect love, alters both our conventional views of love and perception of others.

On the other hand, that particular kind of love which is experienced by a fictional character in *The Unicorn* (and testified to in at least three other sources) leads to a reinterpretation of the traditional doctrines. I am convinced that the experience of perfect love has the power to revitalize traditional doctrines, which now seem remote and unrelated to our concerns and interests. The Trinity and traditional studies of Christology seem utterly remote even to many present-day theologians, Biblical scholars, and theological students. The geography of God, so to speak, matters not a whit to their experiences, their problems, concerns, and worries. To see these doctrines in relation to the view of love Murdoch and others have described not only makes them seem relevant to us but, more than that, the doctrines so interpreted become bearers of life-giving experience, direction, and understanding. They matter, and tell us something we did not know and that we now want to know, something the sheer experience of love does not itself tell us.

My proposal then is to deny that the common viewpoint, which leaves no room for God in the universe, is the only one, and to claim that the issue is to get oneself into a position whereby one can perceive the presence of God permeating both the natural and human environment. *What* is seen from this perspective is reality; it is not to be thought of as non-objective or as the internal dynamics of the self projected, but it is the way the world is indeed perceived from that point of view. It is not "objective" in the sense that it can be perceived without getting into a position to perceive it; so the fear that religion will be reduced from a relationship to God to ordinary or scientific truths is avoided. Yet what is perceived, is perceived, and is claimed to be reality, even if unintegrated with what one presently sees from another perspective. Our view of what is possible has been too narrow, and hence the recognition of God's presence has been thwarted. There has been a conventional secularity (a self-contained universe), as well as a conventional religion, and both shut us off from the cultivation of needs and questions which enable us to get into a position to recognize the presence of God.

Chapter Two

THE EXPERIENCE OF
PERFECT LOVE

*

All of us rightly believe that we know what love is; we have experienced it in one form or another. But most of us have experienced it only to a limited degree or in less than a perfect form. Perfect love is a rare experience; we all crave to be properly loved, yet such love usually eludes us.

It is my conviction that if perfect love is portrayed well, it can be brought closer to our concrete daily experiences, and we can reach toward it through these ordinary daily experiences. So my procedure here will be to present an experience of perfect love which occurs to a character in a novel. It will enable us to see what perfect love is and why it is so difficult to enter and to remain in that kind of relationship. Once this has been done we will, in the rest of this book, see how God's love comes to us and how we may enter into it.

SECTION I

The experience comes to the character Effingham Cooper in Iris Murdoch's novel *The Unicorn*. He is an intelligent and successful civil servant, in the prime of life. Through a series of mishaps, he becomes utterly and hopelessly lost in a remote and desolate place during his annual visit to the home of his friend and former tutor. Rather stupidly he gets himself trapped in a bog, and finding himself slowly sinking, he realizes that there is no realistic hope of rescue. The author then describes an experience which occurs to this extremely vain man, who had never really quite grown up, as he confronts for the first time the fact of his death.

. . . The confrontation brought with it a new quietness and a new terror. The dark bog seemed empty now, utterly empty, as if, because of the great mystery which was about to be enacted, the little wicked gods had withdrawn. Even the stars were veiled now, and Effingham was at the centre of a black globe. He felt the touch of some degraded, gibbering panic. He could still feel himself slowly sinking. He could not envisage what was to come. He did not want to perish whimpering. As if obeying some imperative, a larger imperative than he had ever acknowledged before, he collected himself and concentrated his attention; yet what he was concentrating on was blackness too, a very dark central blackness. He began to feel dazed and light-headed.

Max [his friend and former tutor] had always known about death, had always sat there like a judge in his chair, facing towards death, like a judge or like a victim. Why had Effingham never realized that this was the only fact that mattered, perhaps the only fact there was? If one had realized this, one could have lived all one's life in the light. Yet why in the light, and why did it seem now that the dark ball at which he was staring was full of light? Something had been withdrawn, had slipped away from him in the moment of his attention, and that something was simply himself. Perhaps he was dead already, the darkening image of the self forever removed. Yet what was left, for something was surely left, something existed still? It came to him with the simplicity of a simple sum. What was left was everything else, all that was not himself, that object which he had never before seen and upon which he now gazed with the passion of a lover. And indeed he could always have known this, for the fact of death stretches the length of life. Since he was mortal he was nothing, and since he was nothing all that was not himself was filled to the brim with being, and it was from this that the light streamed. This then was love, to look and look until one exists no more, *this* was the love which was the same as death. He looked and knew, with a clarity which was one with the increasing light, that with the death of the self the world becomes quite automatically the object of a perfect love. He clung to the words "quite automatically" and murmured them to himself as a charm.

Something gave way under his right leg. . . . There was nothing firm, and his hands plunged desperately about in the mud. . . . He was now fixed in the bog almost to the waist and sinking faster. The final panic came. He uttered several low cries and then a loud terrified shrieking wail, the voice of total despair at last.[1]

It is somewhat surprising that Effingham Cooper should have the experience of perfect love, for he is a colossal egotist, who imagines himself to be loved by various women and who is himself apparently incapable of a realistic love for anyone. Yet it is precisely this feature of his person, that he has hitherto been unable to perceive the reality of other people and things, which sharply brings out the fundamental feature of love, namely, the recognition or perception of something besides oneself. It is by facing the fact of death for the first time that he escapes for a moment from the blindness caused by his self-concern (what "had slipped away . . . was simply himself"). As a result, he sees for the first time the reality of other things, "that object which he had never before seen." And that recognition of "all that was not himself" as independent, utterly and totally independent of himself, yet captivating his attention completely, is said to be love. To see reality is to love it, quite automatically; it is not by any act of will; one is drawn or compelled by the object.

This experience of love is something that happened to him; he did not seek it, prepare for it, or apparently even know that such an experience was possible. The novelist stresses that it occurred "quite automatically." And even though the novelist also stresses that it is through death or because of a realization of one's own death that the perception of others as realities occurred, I do not believe that this is to be interpreted as meaning that it occurs by ceasing to be; for even though death is imminent, Effingham still does exist and he is conscious, since he is aware of other things. He is not, however, self-conscious.

He is so full of the presence and reality of something else that his own presence is not part of his awareness (". . . to look and look until one exists no more, *this* was the love which was the same as death"). The nearness of death enabled him to become full of the presence of other things and to lack self-consciousness because by its nearness he became aware that he had no power or control over them. He will die and cease to have power over anything, and yet other things will continue to be. They thus become recognized as realities because they are independent, utterly independent of himself. This is the death of the self as the one reality, the only reality one recognizes, with all else subordinate, orbiting about oneself, having significance and value assigned unrealistically because assigned primarily in terms of its relation to oneself.

It is the withdrawal of power or control, then, which is fundamental to a recognition of the independence of things, and with their independence, they can confront him with a compelling, beauteous radiance. To become aware of death is to become aware of his lack of power, not only now in a bog, but a lack of power that has always been. Now that he feels helpless in the bog, he sees that in reality he has *always* been helpless over things; that is, there has always been something which was not himself, not in orbit around him, not to be controlled by being only so perceived. The fact of death can tell one this, as it did Effingham, but confronting death is only a means to the more important fact that it is because one has the power to perceive all things with oneself as their center that one is prevented from the perception of things as independent of oneself. One has only to cease to exert one's power to be a center to accept them fully as independent realities, to live "in the light." Failure to allow other things to be outside the self distorts one's awareness of them. If they are not independent, their glorious radiance and preciousness are unperceived.

The stress on power and independence in the analysis of this passage finds some support in a letter which apparently refers to the same view of love by an actual, in contrast to a fictional, person, and one moreover who powerfully influenced the author of *The Unicorn.*

> We have to distinguish between three domains. First that which is absolutely independent of us; it includes all the accomplished facts in the whole universe at the moment, and everything which is happening or going to happen later beyond our reach. In this domain everything which comes about is in accordance with the will of God, without any exception. Here then we must love absolutely everything, as a whole and in each detail, including evil in all its forms; notably our own past sins, in so far as they are past (for we must hate them in so far as their root is still present), our own sufferings, past, present and to come, and—what is by far the most difficult—the sufferings of other men in so far as we are not called upon to relieve them.[2]

Here Simone Weil describes what I take to be basically the same perception and love as the character Effingham Cooper experienced; we must love that "which is absolutely independent of us." One does recognize differences between what is good and evil, suffering and happiness. But Simone Weil writes that we are to love them nonetheless; that is, we are not to allow our tastes, desires, preferences, notions of utility, or even our moral judgments to prevent our loving them. These are not removed in the sense that one can be said, for example, to enjoy suffering or to fail to notice that something is useful or useless. But they are not to blind one to perceiving their independence of one's evaluation of them on such bases, however valid and sound those evaluations and bases may be. In the domain of things which have an "absolute independence," to remove the self is to prevent the operation of our tastes, desires, ideas of utility and the rest from keeping us from also seeing things as independent of them. As they are, whether useless or useful, good or bad, painful or pleasant, they are to be loved, as a whole and in each detail, because they are there. One's love is a mark that one has perceived them independently of their relation to oneself and various standards.

Section II

We now want to specify some problems this experience raises and to resolve them. We may begin by asking whether there really is such a perception of the independence of things as was attributed to this fictional character. We know that there are other things besides ourselves. We do handle and see other things on a vast number of occasions and in innumerable circumstances, and in theory we know this or realize this. But how can we show that there is a particular sort of experience, an experience of the independence of other things, and that it is the retention of our control over them which keeps us from having the experience of their reality and of perfect love? That the problem is especially difficult can be immediately indicated by the fact that the experience is extremely difficult to come by. The very unusual circumstances in which it occurred to Effingham Cooper suggest this; not many people in the prime of life so unexpectedly stand on the brink of death, with the time to face their death, without the distraction of pain or the weakness and weariness produced by illness to prevent the concentration of their attention. Panic, which would paralyze reflection, is brought under control. ("He felt the touch of some degraded, gibbering panic. . . . As if obeying some imperative, a larger imperative than he had ever acknowledged before, he collected himself and concentrated his attention; . . .").[3] It would therefore take a great deal to seek to verify that there is such an experience of independence and of love by the re-production of these circumstances; and as far as this experience is concerned, it would be pointless to make an empirical survey to find out what people experience while dying or when thinking about death, or whether they have ever had such an experience.

The unusualness of the experience is further suggested by the fact that Simone Weil is a saintly person. Her ability to perceive as she did was apparently the hard-won privilege of a saint. Not only did it take contemplation, reflection, and self-examination, but it required also the deliberate and painful placing of herself in circumstances and conditions not commonly experienced by academic people so as to be able to view things from these perspectives. She took a job in the Renault Works for a year, worked in the fields during the harvest, and refused the extra nourishment ordered by doctors during the Second World War because she desired to share the hardships of those she had left behind in France.

Yet the very unusualness of the experience, which causes difficulties for the confirmation of its existence, also enables us to see that, as recorded in the case of Effingham, it is the acme or the highest degree of the recognition of the reality of others; it is *perfect* love, with the *total* removal of one's self. We should bear in mind that Simone Weil said that all things absolutely independent of us *must* be loved; she did not claim that she actually did love them, or always did love them.

The extreme difficulty of coming by the experience of perfect love suggests then that it is to be regarded as a *goal* to be attained, and as an extraordinarily difficult one.

The difficulty is well worth emphasizing by giving still another instance of its occurrence. Laurens van der Post recounts the experience in a prisoner of war camp of men who in the closing months of the war fully expected to be slaughtered by their captors.

> It was amazing how often and how many of my men would confess to me, after some Japanese excess worse than usual, that for the first time in their lives they had realized the truth, and the dynamic liberating power of the first of the Crucifixion utterances: "Forgive them for they know not what they do."
>
> I found the moment they grasped this fundamental fact of our prison situation, forgiveness became a product not of an act of will or of personal virtue even, but an automatic and all-compelling consequence of a law of understanding: as real and indestructible as Newton's law of gravity. The tables of the spirit would be strangely and promptly turned and we would find ourselves without self-pity of any kind, feeling deeply sorry for the Japanese as if we were the free men and they the

prisoners—men held in some profound *oubliette* of their own minds.[4]

Because it is a goal to be attained we need not, therefore, have had the experience in the sense of a sudden eruption, as in Effingham's case, or as a pervasive and deep awareness (even if not complete) as in Simone Weil's case to recognize what is being portrayed. Some degree of recognition of other things—realizing in an argument the validity of another point of view, a scholar not twisting data, absorption in the presence of a child, or in the beauty of natural objects—enables one to extend the line of vision toward the ideal case, the perfect recognition of other things.

Granted then that we can form some idea of the experience of perfect love without having had it ourselves, we need to show that it would occur were we to relinquish our power or control over things. We can do this by showing that the self does distort perception and that the way we usually experience things is not the way they are: that there is a contrast between what is the case and the way we experience it. Then we can say that, because our present experience of things is distorted, *there is a more appropriate way to experience things.* Precisely what that experience is like, we ourselves cannot tell without its occurrence; we have only a glimpse of it to the extent that something is perceived as being independent of us, as when we see another person's point of view, and the extension of this to the ideal case as described by a few. But we know that there is a more appropriate way to experience things since we know our present way is distorted. And because it is by the exercise of our power that our present perception is distorted, the experience or perception would occur were our power or control relinquished.

Let us then consider how the self distorts perception. There is of course a considerable body of empirical data which shows that our perception is affected by such things as expectations, emotional conflicts, and stress, and there are experiments which seek to measure their effects with precision.[5] There are also theories, such as Freud's, which put great emphasis on unconscious desires over which we do not have much control, attempts to gratify them in a physical and social environment which is not always amenable to their gratification, and the role of fantasy as a major means of controlling and satisfying them. It seems to me that Murdoch (in her second essay in *The Sovereignty of Good*, pp. 51–54) endorses the basic picture of powerful internal forces, extremely difficult to control, and fantasy as major hindrances to correct perception of other things.

My own claims about distortion in our perception do not rest upon either empirical studies of perception or Freudian-type views. It hinges on the fact that each of us is a conscious center,[6] aware of how his body feels, and with an unreflective concern for himself which is enormous. We usually perceive everything from the perspective of ourselves; in terms of how it affects us. However small a portion of the universe in space and time we occupy, and however limited our social position may be, each of us is a reality in contact with and variously related to numerous other things, both human and nonhuman. Since we are centers of consciousness, each with a body calling attention to itself, with all sorts of emotions and feelings, placed in contact with many outside things, we have very good reason indeed to turn our attention to ourselves and be preoccupied with ourselves. We do have ourselves to look out for, and we are aware of pressures on us.

We have, in addition, the power to occupy a position which is a type of solipsism; that is, when we have a *unique* concern for ourselves, we thereby see things from our selves as the center and estimate the value and significance of all things in terms of their worth for us. Their value is conditional; our own is not. We are an end and nothing else is so perceived or regarded. We are not only ontologically primary, since our concern is for ourselves and for other things only as they relate to ourselves, but we are ontologically unique, since there is no experience of other centers as centers (in the case of people, animals, plants) and no regard for nonliving things as existing independently of their relation to us and of their value or significance to us. We can then occupy the stance of this type of solipsism, and while occupying it, truly say that there are other minds, other things feel, and things exist independently of us, yet be *experiential* solipsists.[7]

But this position is a distortion, for each of us is but one item among many; each of us is not the center of the universe, but only one focus. Other items exist independently of us and so their significance and value is not to be measured solely in terms of their relation to ourselves. As a power, each of us is a center; and we register the impingement of other things on ourselves. But we have the capacity to keep from recognizing other centers as centers and from recognizing any item as independent of ourselves. Our power is not to be measured solely in terms of our physical strength or the ability to get what we want through our influence on others, but also in terms of our beliefs, our evaluations, and our imagination. For example, Effingham Cooper believed that almost every woman he met was in love with him. He misinterpreted their actions and played out in his fantasy how miserable they must feel over his lack of response to their affection, and so acted toward them with a self-satisfied solicitude. The indifference felt toward him, even the rejection in one instance, he did not perceive. We can thus handle all that is not us in such a way that we can remain unique centers. Reality is distorted not simply because we register the impingement of things on us and so are conscious of ourselves as centers and because we have self-concern, but because we can *occupy* a *unique* center; because we have the power to occupy that position and to hold it intact in face of the fact that there is a world independent of us containing other centers somewhat like ourselves.[8] We can keep things in orbit around ourselves and not release them. Such a position is unrealistic since they in fact are not in orbit around us.

This view of our power to prevent ourselves from recognizing the reality of other things allows us to draw a distinction between two kinds of self, or what I will call a *de facto* person and a moral person. We can also identify the factors which make it difficult to perceive reality and to sustain such a perception. To be a *de facto* person is to have a unique self-regard, and thereby to judge all things only as they relate to oneself. As I have said above, the self of each of us looms so large and is so pervasive that we do not perceive or experience the most obvious truth, the utter independence from us of other things. One does not actually experience oneself as standing in the relationship of but one among others, one item among many. We do not as *de facto* persons experience or have ontological humility.

A moral person is one who is aware that he is but one reality among other realities. It is not at all clear to me that anyone is able to occupy that position, that is, to perceive others as realities and to remain in that relation to them all the time, or even for very long or very often. I recall, for example, being very conscious of a five-year-old son and thinking how he was a center like myself, and feeling very pleased about my moral achievement. Suddenly he bit me, and I reacted by hitting him very hard. In an instant I had reverted to seeing things from my own perspective and reacting automatically to another person with myself as the center. Nonetheless one can be aware of the idea of what a moral person is, and at times become aware to a degree of what a saintly person such as Simone Weil experienced or what the character Effingham experienced powerfully and with extraordinary clarity. To grasp even the idea of what a moral person is, is to approach being a moral person; it is to move toward a more realistic relation to others. It is more realistic because some of the distortion of the original position has been removed.

But the idea of a moral person or a moral perception, ideally represented in the experience of Effingham Cooper, though it deflates oneself as one is moved from the *de facto* position of vision, has the "quite automatic" effect of revealing the preciousness of other things.[9] Perceived as realities, they grip one in fascination and adoration. They appear so extraordinarily worthy and absorbing that one's awareness is fully occupied by them. One's fantastic distortion and unrealistic self-evaluation is now shed, but one does not oneself become valueless. Without becoming engaged in narcissistic self-love, one can become aware that one is worthy as well. Since one is a reality oneself, one can rightly become the object of another's perception and thereby the object of another's love. One's true value is perceived by another. One has worth, true worth: the same worth as other things. How much, need not be here examined, but nobility is suggested by the very fascination one thing can have for another.[10]

People often have a very low estimate of their worth. The great success of a book like *I'm OK, You're OK* suggests how widespread the feeling of low self-esteem is. Sermons preached on the idea that we are full of pride do not ring true, because only a few people feel as though they are great successes. Our society reserves high praise for only the exceptional, those who are at the top or near the top of their profession or endeavor. So almost everyone else has to wrestle with the idea that he or she has not achieved as much as one ought in a society that claims to offer everyone the opportunity to get to the top.

On the one hand, low self-esteem prevents us from perceiving our true worth; and we will have much to say later about recognizing ourselves as persons loved and valued with a perfect love. On the other hand, we can have a low opinion of ourselves, even self-hatred, and still have a unique *de facto* self-regard and self-concern. Our anger and disappointment with ourselves because we fail to achieve success according to the scale of values of our society is an anger and disappointment precisely because we do so care about ourselves. And that anger and disappointment are blinding because we do not see that there are other centers like ourselves. So a *de facto* position is not to be confused with pride, or feelings of satisfaction. It is quite compatible with very negative feelings about oneself.

It is often said from the pulpit and in popular psychology that one must first love oneself and only after that is it possible to love others. But to shed negative feelings about oneself and to affirm oneself are not necessarily to have escaped from a *de facto* position. One can attain self-love and then develop positive feelings toward others, and still perceive all things as though they were in orbit around oneself.

"Love your neighbor as yourself" is often interpreted to mean: Jesus tells us that self-love is all right. That in fact you must love yourself if you are to love your neighbor, because you are to love him *as you love yourself.* But actually the commandment means that one is to have the same unreflective concern for others as one *already* and uniquely has for oneself. No one has to be taught to have self-concern; no one has to develop it. It is there and is all-encompassing. What must take place is for one to shed that unique self-concern so that one may recognize the reality of others with that immediate, unreflective, untaught concern which one now has only for oneself.

SECTION III

Why is it difficult to move from seeing things from our own perspective? That is, why is it difficult to move from a *de facto* to a moral perspective, and thereby to see the worth of others and to recognize our own true worth? Why, in other words, is it so difficult to love and to be loved?

A major reason is that a person does have a point of view. Because I am a feeling center and care for myself, with other things pressing on me, I keep attending to myself. The frequency and intensity of the impingement of other things on me, and my unique self-love and self-concern, keep me from losing my self-awareness for an awareness of others. (We will develop this more fully in a moment.)

In addition, the recognition of one's true worth and the loss of an inflated self-concern are dependent on others. For example, I had had a very good education prior to going to seminary. So I felt superior to my fellow students and even to some of my professors. It was not long before I was isolated and without friends. That painful isolation taught me a great deal, and I returned the next year a somewhat chastened person. I looked forward to establishing a new relationship with others. But no one noticed the change in me. Everyone treated me the same way. So the sheer loss or partial removal of an exaggerated self-worth is not enough.

In becoming a moral person one does not directly perceive one's own worth at all. In the moral position one is fully occupied with the perception of others. Others may perceive me, love me,[11] and thereby my true worth be recognized by them. Even so, I may not be aware of their perception of me. For that, I must, in perceiving them, be aware that they are perceiving me and recognize my effect on them. I *indirectly* perceive my worth in my effect on them. To become aware of my true worth, I must be occupied fully by them (and they by me), and see myself only in my effect on them. To receive moral worth (to perceive myself as a moral person) thus is structurally complex. But it is further complicated by the fact that in reality one is indeed lovable or one has worth. So there is a reality-basis, so to speak, or a sound ground for the *de facto* worth and concern with which we regard ourselves. Although to become aware of my worth in true and accurate measure I must give up my *de facto* absorption with myself as the only center, the fact that I have some genuine worth, and am one who is conscious and concerned for myself, gives me *reason* to use my power to *retain* my focus on myself and to contemplate and honor my own worth. We can get stuck on recognition of our genuine, though distortedly perceived, worth, and thereby inflate it and not see others or a true perception of it. Our very worth then is another factor which prevents us from perceiving the worth of others.

Closely related to this is the fact first mentioned, that we, simply as centers, are in contact with other centers. People as they impinge on each other conflict. For the very relation of other people to us, when they occupy a *de facto* position, is a violation of our true worth (even should they value us very highly for, say, our cleverness, usefulness to them, etc.). For example, even should we have an employer who is by generally accepted standards a good one, nonetheless our value for him is largely seen in terms of our contribution to the success of the business. Once we cease to be an asset, the treatment of us changes drastically. We are viewed from a point of view that does not see us as a center. We are not recognized as an independent reality. Our worth is violated; and there are grounds to resist this exercise of power over us, whether we ourselves occupy the *de facto* or moral position; for in both we have worth, even though our true worth is distorted by our own *de facto* self-concern.

The way we resist or react to being regarded by others from a *de facto* position will differ drastically according to which of the two positions we occupy. For example, the employee can refuse to recognize that in a business enterprise one is bound to be judged in part by what one contributes toward its success. This fact is not wiped out by the employer's failure to recognize you as a center. But if you react solely from your own point of view, you fail to see this fact, or do not give it its due weight, and you may regard your boss as a totally calculating person. You may then treat him with contempt (always keeping it just within the bounds he will tolerate) which really is a way to get back at him. When we react as centers trying to get the other person into our orbit or control, the response and counter-response of *de facto* relations can spiral indefinitely.

We can also react from a moral position, and one type of moral response can be the sacrifice of ourselves to the other. We realize that in any enterprise we are bound to be regarded at least in part for our utility. This is a sacrifice because something of worth, and known to be of genuine worth, is given up and because it includes our recognition and acceptance of the reality of the other, who as an employer must take utility into account. This response would be to love our suffering.

A moral response does not by any means exclude all resistance. We can both make sacrifices of our selves and also resist outrage to our persons. For example, I knew a department chairman who avoided his share of menial tasks, such as taking his turn at registration when students had to be enrolled for courses. He asked a member of the department if she would mind staying on a few extra hours to finish up the job. The woman was a former nun and, thinking she was acting out of love, said yes. The response, though well intended, was inappropriate. He should have been turned down, for he was not helped by her kindness to recognize the reality of others, but was simply taking advantage of her.

We are so unused to love and resistance being joined that I will give another example of the way resistance to the outrage of our genuine worth is a moral response. One day in a drugstore, while waiting in a long line at a check-out counter, I was talking with a young couple just in front of me. When their turn came and all their purchases were totaled up, the wife handed over a charge card. The check-out lady became furious, shouted that charge cards had to be taken to another register. She was indeed busy, but this hardly excused the way she ripped into this couple, who meekly gathered up their goods, apologizing profusely. They should, I believe, have resisted this outrage (and in fact I should have resisted on their behalf when they failed to); for this person should have had it called to her attention that, however busy she was, these people had acted in ignorance, and were centers of feeling too. "Wait a minute. There is no sign or any other way to tell that you don't honor your own credit cards at this cash register." This sort of reaction was called for, as a minimum. Instead, by caving in to her point of view, they had not only sacrificed themselves, but they had failed in their responsibility to her: the responsibility to call her attention to the fact that they were people. They had failed to help her break out of her perception of others solely from her point of view.

People, then, are in conflict; that is, each seeks to put or to keep the other in orbit around himself. This enormously hampers one's ability to move from a *de facto* position to a regard for others as realities. For the overwhelmingly common situation is to be pressed on by other centers and forces, and to impinge on others and get reactions from them. Effingham Cooper's position of passiveness or suspension of power is most unusual. For a short period of time, by being trapped in a bog, he loses his physical power over other things. He could have pretended that there would be a rescue and kept his mind on that, and spun fantasies about it, or spent his time yelling his head off for help, as he was tempted to. Instead, with his physical powers reduced virtually to nil, he is able to perceive his nothingness in the sense that he recognizes that things have always been independent of him. This profound resignation of himself, of his power and *de facto* worth, cannot, however, be sustained. His final cry in utter despair is heard, and a native of the region, who is experienced in its ways, is able to save him from death. As the novelist shows, Effingham is unable to sustain his loving relation with others. Upon his rescue, he is tucked into bed in a fussy, but humorous, manner by three women, who are all united in his delirious perception as a single golden fuzz.[12] What he perceived in the bog as one object, gleaming with radiance, fragments into particulars, each now a separate power, as the three women symbolically and literally united for a moment in a joint concern for him—and he united to them in response to their affection—separate into different centers. The experience and vision both in the bog and of the single golden orb of three women looking after him solicitously fade and such unity seems silly, certainly silly when put into words.

His profound resignation is not only momentary but it seems that such resignation cannot simply be willed; that is, one cannot simply give up oneself as a power and be passive in relation to other powers. The heroine, to whom the title *The Unicorn* refers, is intended to show this. In many legends the unicorn is a fierce beast, but Christianity has made it gentle and ready for self-sacrifice. The heroine apparently has become gentle and has sacrificed herself. She has lived for seven years in self-exile in a remote region, self-bound to the small grounds of the house,

apparently in penitence for unfaithfulness to her lionlike husband and her violent and nearly successful attempt to murder
him. Ostensibly she has now withdrawn herself, her power; she
has in this sense died. But in this very position of apparent
withdrawal and sacrifice, she holds a host of other people on
tenterhooks around her in an absurd and unrealistic situation.
She remains a center, the center, and her willful ostensive withdrawal, which is not truly a withdrawal, ultimately brings destruction to many of those in orbit around her as they, for their
own purposes, seek to protect her, free her, or possess her.[13]

One does have power; one cannot escape from this and
continue to exist. The momentary vision, whereby one resigns
one's control over all and suspends one's power to be the only
reality, does not solve the problem of escape from the unreality
of being a *de facto* person, nor does a willful self-surrender,
sacrifice, or withdrawal. This passiveness is a shutting of one's
eyes, as though there were no other centers of consciousness to
tread on, or run up against, and above all denying the tremendous power that is oneself because one fears that one cannot
control it. Withdrawal from the world, from contact with other
powers, is not possible. To have made such a withdrawal is not
to have stripped away the *de facto* self any more than a monk
or twice-born Christian has destroyed the root of sin. In fact, to
try it can be terribly dangerous, as one has not really resigned
oneself, even if one sincerely tries to and if one suffers for it.

An account has now been given of what we mean by perfect
love, why we think there is such an experience (even though it
is recognizable by most of us only by experience of it to a small
degree), and the difficulties of attaining and sustaining it because we are centers of power and because of the uses of our
power. Something of its importance has been indicated, since
it is a truer experience of others, of oneself, and a more realistic
relation to other things, but we will have much more to say
about its religious importance in the next chapter.

It should be well noted that there has been no attempt to
explain human behavior or motivation by the concepts of a *de
facto* and a moral person. These are ways to classify and to

evaluate our *perceptions*. Some suggestions have been made about how we put things into orbit about us: by fantasy and self-deception. But what is crucial is not the means I have mentioned but the fact that we can and do put things into orbit around ourselves. Likewise, what would motivate us to move from a *de facto* to a moral position has not been considered; all that has been done in this regard is to give some of the factors which make it difficult to move from that position and to recognize others' and one's own true worth.

Of course, this classification of our perceptions can be extended derivatively to our behavior. Behavior can be classified as that which enables us to retain a *de facto* position or to move toward a moral one. The concepts of *de facto* and moral positions of perception, then, allow us to judge people and their behavior; one can evaluate one's self and, with a goal to be attained, a society's and one's own progress and development.

A major concern in the next chapter will be to develop a view which combines a very high and rigorous standard of judgment of people's perception and behavior with a merciful but unsentimental regard for others and oneself. For even though the classifications of *de facto* and moral are sharp, and the ideal is the genuine position to be in, we are to move toward the ideal in degrees, and to judge people on the basis of the progress they are making toward the achievement of the ideal. For as will be shown, attainment of the ideal is not possible in this life, and moreover, precisely what it would be like to live the ideal in a sustained fashion is at present not fully conceivable. For as we will see, the ideal is the kind of life found in the Trinity, an indwelling of several centers in unity. We have not as yet, however, completed our delineation of what perfect love is. There is still another feature to be considered, to which we will now turn.

Section IV

No distinctions have been made between those things which we perceive. With Effingham "all that was not himself" is called "that object"; it is as though it were one thing and all of it is to

be loved passionately. In the passage from Simone Weil, everything that is absolutely independent of us is to be loved, and she
explicitly mentions that this includes evil, our own sins, and our
own and others' sufferings. The moral position is such that distinctions between good and evil, suffering and happiness, even
when the distinctions are recognized, do not affect the require-
ment that they are to be loved. We find the same thing in a
sermon by J. R. Jones, where Coleridge's Ancient Mariner
looked at

> . . . the slimy things which infested the water round the ship,
> and he began to be *aware* of them. . . . Something then welled
> up within him to which he could only give the name of 'love'
> and he *suddenly felt grateful for them.* Not because they were
> of any use to him, because they were not; and not necessarily
> because he *liked* them: he found them strangely beautiful but
> possibly not attractive. The experience was something quite
> different from this—it was a gratitude for their existence.[14]

Jones then also notes the absence of concern with distinctions, ones which divide things according to our own views of
their utility, potential for exploitation, or attractiveness. They
are irreducible to these standards (they can be so viewed, and
hence reduced, but they can break these bounds and enable us
to see that they are not truly reducible). To see them as independent of one's self, with their own particularity, is to see their
unconditional preciousness.

But there are distinctions between them. The distinctions
which are not only perceived but are also of concern from the
moral point of view are: (1) their particularity (as we have already suggested), and (2) their vulnerability. To regard them
simply as they are, perhaps useless and even unattractive to
oneself, and yet not to wish them otherwise but to be thankful
for them as they are, is to allow them independence of oneself.
To allow them to be as they are, and precious as they are, is to
recognize their particularity, and their value as particulars.[15]
Simone Weil expresses this in relation to people.

> I have the essential need, and I think I can say the vocation, to
> move among men of every class and complexion, mixing with

them and sharing their life and outlook, so far that is to say as
conscience allows, merging into the crowd and disappearing
among them, so that they show themselves as they are, putting
off all disguises with me. It is because I long to know them, so
as to love them just as they are. For if I do not love them as they
are, it will not be they whom I love, and my love will be unreal.
I do not speak of helping them, because as far as that goes I am
unfortunately quite incapable of doing anything as yet.[16]

To perceive the detailed common stuff as it is, unadorned by
the glamor we can throw over it, and not to be affected by the
desire to wish it otherwise, is to perceive it as particulars, independent and so loved. But the note of "helping them" introduces an element of discord. For as Jones points out, one of
the features of what we see when free of what I have called the
de facto position is its extreme vulnerability.

To love a thing is to see a thing as existing in its own right—to
go out to its existence. And to go out to a thing in this way when
it is a living thing, and particularly when it is a living person,
is *fundamentally to have pity for it.* . . . For the insight into its
existence which makes us rejoice in its existence is at the same
time an insight into its suffering, its defencelessness, its profound vulnerability.[17]

To see something as vulnerable and suffering is to see it as
a particular; its own condition is important. And its condition is
one of need. The moral vision is not simply that all else is
independent of oneself, to be seen as it is in its own particularity, and loved as it is; but in the case of living things, there
is a recognition of its internality. The object is seen to be incomplete, suffering, and vulnerable. There is the recognition of
what it is like to be the object whose independence we recognize, and which from the outside is seen to be gloriously radiant.[18]

We can illustrate what it is like to be a particular by reference to another of Iris Murdoch's novels, *The Time of the Angels.*[19] We can only illustrate this point because by necessity
particulars are particulars, so what it is like to be one cannot be
fully presented by giving any single case. Yet though particulars
are vulnerable in different ways, and each suffers in its own way,

we can nonetheless illustrate with one particular that to be a particular is to want to be recognized as one, to be recognized as oneself. This is the same as the need to be loved. We mentioned this earlier, schematically, when it was pointed out that to be perceived by others from their *de facto* position is to be outraged and to have one's true worth violated. This structural feature of our analysis is the principle by which we have selected the need to be loved from all the possible material one could relate under the rubric "what it is like to be a particular."

The central figure in this novel is Pattie O'Driscoll. She is black, or at least half-black. Her mother was an Irish prostitute, and because Pattie is black, her mother figures that she must be the daughter of a West Indian she vaguely remembers. Pattie for some years now has been the servant of an Anglican priest who, as the book opens, has just moved into a new rectory in London. It is a strange parish. All but the tower of the church had been destroyed by bombs during the last war and even it is scheduled to be pulled down. There are virtually no residences left in the area. Since there is no work to be done, the bishop uses it as a post for his problem children and this priest is one. The porter in the rectory, who keeps the inadequate heating system going and nothing else, is a Russian exile. Some of the other characters are a daughter of the priest, his niece, his brother, the son of the porter, and a conventional retired headmistress. The author cares about the relationships between these people; every relationship between them is important, and virtually every one of them has a relationship with the others. But the main ones in the book are those between Pattie and the priest and Pattie and the porter.[20]

Pattie was given to an orphanage by her mother. She is an island: alone and miserable for it. She is cut off from a father she never knew, and a mother who gives her up and dies. She has no one. Her blackness in a white country is to stress her isolation, and even when she grows up she has no sense of identification with blacks she sees (she does not know any). What she craves and never had in the orphanage is for someone to love her. She was well treated in the orphanage—fed well, clothed well, sent to school, and always treated kindly. But no one ever saw her, just her. Only when she was a baby and a small child did her mother hold and caress her, sob over her in drunken fits. It was she, she who was addressed and held. That one little spark of animal love is all she had; otherwise, she had not been truly touched.

Now the relations of the priest to Pattie and the porter to Pattie exhibit different kinds of love and the effect of different kinds of love on Pattie. She left domestic service with her first employers (good, enlightened people, who did a lot for her but who did not break her miserable isolation) to enter the same employment with the priest. Immediately he opened himself to her. He spoke in a fond way to her, he touched her, he could see her, and she began to blossom. He did this naturally and easily, and in the same fashion, one day, he took her to bed. By the time they move to London, the bubble has burst for Pattie. He does not marry Pattie, even though his wife is now dead; the daughter and niece, who are members of the household, hate Pattie, for what has passed between herself and the priest. Even the priest no longer takes her to bed. Once again, she is alone, more painfully aware of her loneliness than ever. She is now enslaved, hanging onto him who alone once made her feel alive, and yet it is a relationship that is destroying her. She is now passively dependent on him, without the slightest incentive (save some daydreams which she recognizes as such); deeply guilty for the injury she inflicted on the priest's now dead wife; and painfully aware of the enmity of the girls.

In London, she meets the porter. The novel beautifully describes how slowly and painfully she, and for that matter he, begin to come to life. He too is an outcast, a refugee from Russia. From a wealthy home, he has been reduced to being a porter, with only one tangible shred of his past, a tremendous icon of the blessed Trinity. He is not religious, but it stands in his room and from it he somehow draws strength. Through it he has a living relationship to a past, a vague past, but nonetheless an artery through which blood still flows.

He is able to see Pattie—to see *her*—for he has never become part of or understood English culture, and so he cannot place or pigeonhole her. He has to take her as he finds her. Every little thing she has done interests him. He wants to hear it, and to tell her about himself; that is to say, she matters to him. And so, slowly as they have a cup of tea and talk each day, she begins to come to life, because she is loved. She is perceived as existing, as a reality, as a center. She is no longer unattached; she can begin to think of a future (and one not wholly based on fantasy as before). They will go one day to visit the sea (she had never seen it); they will be married.

Then the priest realizes what is happening. He is losing Pattie (her slavery is ending), so he takes her to bed again. This snaps the tie with the porter; it hurts him, but it also hurts her. Her need for love, and the priest's power over her, enables her to submit without any resistance, but it degrades her in her own eyes. She realizes that she has been outraged, for she has begun to realize that she has true worth.

Now I want to contrast the effects on Pattie of two kinds of love. She, as we all, needs to be loved and to love: to be so attached. The porter's type of love, as far as it went, was healing and life-giving (but he did not have the courage to continue loving her once the confines of the cozy boiler room setup had been destroyed; he was afraid to venture). The priest's was life-giving too at first, but then it became destructive. Why? The priest's malady is Pattie's malady too: isolation. Pattie started out in life isolated and is struggling to move from it, but the priest is becoming progressively more isolated. He had long since lost the reality of God; he is rapidly ceasing to recognize the reality of others, and is losing the reality of himself as well. He believes, as apparently does Heidegger, whom he reads, in the Abyss and Nothingness. That is, Heidegger draws a sharp distinction between Being and beings. All that we can name, think about, and normally encounter, are beings; but behind them and moving through them, so to speak, is the nameless Being, the Abyss, or Nothing, for it has no name or character. Demythologized, this means that the priest ceases to perceive the significance of particulars; they are but epiphenomenal or trivial appearances of some underlying something. They do not matter; only what underlies them does. You are not to love anything, not even yourself. So he is steadily withdrawing, losing the reality of all things, including himself.

This is perhaps why he tries to destroy Pattie; for he no longer wants to recognize her particularity. He cannot have Pattie and the porter in love, for that affirms their irreducible existence and value. So he takes her to bed, and destroys her relationship to the porter, and thereby her as a particular that counts for someone. But the action is ambivalent. Pattie is the one thread that keeps him tied to particulars and from sinking completely into the Abyss. He says that she will save him; so he wants to keep her. At least this seems to be why, when she does leave him for a job elsewhere, he commits suicide. His hold on her is all that tells him that he exists as a reality, for she does love him. Her ability to leave him means that he ceases to be a reality, and now "Nothing" exists.

Let me now explicitly state what I am using this material to bring out. We have already described what it is to recognize others' reality—their independence of oneself; now we are considering what it is to be a particular reality not in another's orbit. From the standpoint of being a particular, in the case of human beings, there is the need to be loved as one's self and the need to love; without this there is miserable isolation. So even though we are independent realities, there is the need to be related or attached; not related as we are when we regard each other from *de facto* positions, but a relation in which we regard and are regarded as irreducibly and unconditionally valuable. This includes acceptance of the common stuff that we are, our bodies, our coarseness, as well as our aspirations. It is to recognize that those whom we perceive crave to be recognized. It is to see their *de facto* condition and to accept them so, i.e., to love them, for to see them so is to pity them for their terrible craving to be recognized and their unrealistic self-worth.

This need to be attached—to love and be loved as a particular—means that love is creative and healing. Pattie's miserable isolation, her passivity, her lack of identity, her inability to think of a future, begin to evaporate in the warmth of another's even partial recognition of her. Her deep hurt and ache are soothed and she starts to come to life. But the need to be attached can be powerfully destructive as well. It can mean seeking to put other things in orbit around oneself—that is, not recognizing their reality—and so we get the clash of powers each seeking to overcome the other by some form of control. It can be destructive when one seeks to overcome the need to be attached, as in the case of the heroine of *The Unicorn* or in the case of the priest. He tries to cut himself off from others by becoming progressively isolated. He gave up Pattie physically, he became more and more frightening in his idiosyncrasies in his parish, so that his bishop moved him to one that had virtually no parishioners. There he refuses to allow any callers to see him; refuses to talk on the telephone. All realities are to be shut off. His brother after several failures finally manages to see him. During their conversation, the priest slaps him and says, "For a moment you existed." For a moment, a particular reality broke through his isolation, and that very blow was a confession of it, and a distorted but genuine flash of love. But this was only "for a moment." He withdraws again into the Abyss in which no particulars are distinguishable or matter, where finally even he does not, and so he commits suicide—the final and complete act of isolation.

So love is not merely a beautiful thing. The need to be recognized as a particular, and so loved and so attached to others, can be the source of miserable isolation, as in Pattie's case. And the denial of particularity, as in the case of the priest, can be destructive of others and oneself. Though love can be creative, a source of fulfillment, it is a source of great suffering.

All this can be passed over in many ways. One way is to subsume particulars under some outlook or theory which denies them as irreplaceable centers. This occurs in Plato, in Gnosticism, in contemporary philosophy with its neglect of emotions (as we will see shortly) and with its views in ethics which neglect the uniqueness of people and of different social contexts.[21] The social sciences continually seek and must seek to pass beyond the particular to structures and to laws of structures. Here I want to illustrate by reference to Plato what it means to subsume particulars under some general theory which transfers primary importance and worth from particulars to the theory or scheme and regards particulars as if no more were to be said of them that matters, except what the scheme allows to be said of them.

In the *Symposium* we have one of the great classics on the nature of love. Socrates joins some others in the celebration of the triumph of a friend's play. After a feast, for entertainment, each takes a turn in giving an address on love. There are playful antics with lavish praise to love's greatness and glory and so forth. Then it is the turn of Aristophanes. In many ways what he says is funny. He claims that at one time people did not have one head, two arms, two legs and one set of sex organs, but they had double all of these things—sort of grotesque circular back-to-back Siamese twins, except they were one person. One day a terrible thing happened. Everyone was split down the middle and separated from the other half of himself. And all the parts were scattered. So now everyone seeks his lost half.

This playful myth has a terrible pathos. It is a way to suggest that everyone is incomplete, longing for that which will bring him completeness and make him whole again. In this bizarre picture, Aristophanes suggests the tremendous driving power of love, an often uncontrollable, pushing, driving, irrational desire and need.

Then it is Socrates' turn to speak. He begins with his usual disclaimers about his inability to speak well and all the rest. Then he sketches a picture of love as an attraction which begins on a sensuous, physical level but is progressively refined and spiritualized. At first it is all right to love things of physical beauty, such as the human form, but by training, one is to begin to seek the beautiful itself, which is not this or that beautiful thing. Particular beautiful things are but instantiations, partial instantiations of it, but are not beauty itself. One is to seek true beauty by beginning with particulars which by their participation in it are made beautiful and hence lovable. But ideally one is to pass through them to beauty itself.

In the last resort, what is being suggested here denigrates particulars. They are valuable only because of the presence of something else; their own particularity is not primary.[22] I have used the Murdoch material to say that to love is to perceive particulars as irreducible realities not to be put into orbit around oneself nor to be made an example of something else, a specimen of a universal; for them it is the universal which is the real thing, and the particular is real only in so far as it participates in it. What wants to be loved is a particular, a center, full of unrealistic worth but also consisting of true worth which is not exhausted or captured by whatever likeness it has to others.[23]

Chapter Three

GOD'S PERFECT LOVE

*

In this chapter we will employ the concept of love just presented to give an interpretation of several major Christian doctrines, an interpretation which will amount to a religious view of the world. But it could well be asked, Why should we seek to relate to theology the view that love is the genuine recognition of others? Why not leave the experience of love as it is—an experience?

We mentioned in the first chapter a remark made about Martin Buber to the effect that a person who cannot recognize the I-Thou experience Buber depicts has no heart. But the very same people take it that as far as philosophy is concerned there is no more to be said about it. Buber considered it to be of supreme importance, as the orienting truth of the universe. But one can recognize the experience and not elevate what it exhibits to the place of primacy.

Emotions are neglected in philosophy primarily because they apparently are irrelevant to establishing what is true. People's wants, desires, hopes, aspirations, fears, depressions, sense of isolation, and other feelings do not make any difference to what is true of the world about them. Things are true or false irrespective of our feelings; and to allow feelings to intrude on our estimates of what is true or for emotions to be part of the basis for what is said to be true is to be subjective in the bad sense of prejudice. Emotions are not a source of information about the universe, or its workings, nor can they act as a basis for claims about the universe. They are not bearers of truth as are sense perceptions which can tell one what is the case, nor do they serve to establish a conclusion as does reasoned argument. So when philosophers examine theories, arguments, views, claims, and the like to assess their soundness, feelings clearly are items to be excluded from consideration. Human needs, longings, hopes, and feelings are put to one side as material to be dealt with by psychologists or other social scientists, and then promptly forgotten.

The experience of love we have portrayed is more multi-faceted than Buber's I-Thou, but we face the same problem. Without an appropriate view of reality, Effingham Cooper's experience while sinking in a bog, and the experiences of the Ancient Mariner, Simone Weil, and the prisoners of war, are but single experiences among a vast multitude of experiences. How can such an experience be said to deserve special notice? How can one elevate it to supremacy as the orienting truth of life, giving one a goal and a standard for the evaluation of motives, behavior, character, and a society? We need to portray the universe in such a way that love can be said to be central to it, to be its fundamental truth, to reveal its meaning and significance. Such a portrayal is needed in order for one experience among many to be given overriding importance, as the one which allows all others to be ordered in relation to it. Given an appropriate view of reality, we see how it is that the experience is the correct one for people to have as their goal and standard. To give it a setting, then, allows us to understand how that experience may be a bearer of truth.

Iris Murdoch herself does provide a framework for the experience of love, and thereby makes claims about its importance. As we saw, she believes that our *de facto* self-awareness distorts our perception. The experience of perfect love is a bearer of truth precisely because we are but one reality among many

others. The experience of love is thus a more realistic perception and a guide to a more realistic relation to other realities.
In addition, the experience of love which involves the perception of the vulnerability and suffering of living creatures, and
their craving to be loved, is part of her account of *why* one
should elevate perfect love to the position of being the supreme
or guiding truth of our life, so that to occupy a moral position
is our primary task and all activities are to be evaluated ethically. The reason we are to elevate it, then, is that *what* we
perceive compels it; what we see draws us. But to live ethically
does not necessarily mean to live successfully as judged by social
standards, and death wipes out those things we love and us as
well.

This framework, though sound, only gives an account of why
people should make perfect love their fundamental concern; it
does not elevate perfect love to supremacy in the cosmos. People are but one item among many in a vast cosmos; and love
between men and of men toward all that exists is not the same
as the elevation of love which we find in Christianity. There the
entire universe is regarded as conceived in love, sustained by
love, and directed toward the consummation of that love. I seek
to give a framework that elevates love to such cosmic propor-
tions.

An additional reason for giving a framework for the experience of perfect love is that it brings to life what for many are
dead dogmas. Christian doctrines when interpreted in light of
this experience rebound onto that experience, and enhance it.
They restate *what* love is by putting it on a cosmic scale, and
thus enrich our understanding of it. The doctrines then no
longer seem to be merely intellectual abstractions but become
life-giving truths which nourish us and guide us in our daily
tasks. Every moment becomes a time lived in God's presence.

SECTION I

Christianity teaches that God is a creator: the Maker of all
things. This claim has been and is the source of extremely diffi-

cult intellectual problems primarily because God's relation as a
creator to creatures is a unique one. We make things, such as
tables and chairs, out of previously existing materials; but God,
according to Christian doctrine, has no previously existing
material of which to make something new. As Maker of all
things, he makes the material itself; hence, creation is *ex nihilo*.[1]
Furthermore, God *freely* makes the universe. He is under no
necessity or duress to create, such as a lack of fullness or completeness without a universe.

Now why does this matter—creating *ex nihilo* and freely?

The free creation of genuine realities or particulars *ex nihilo*
when interpreted as an act of love yields a very distinctive kind
of love. That he created *ex nihilo* means that once there were
no realities but God.[2] He could have remained alone, for he
lacked nothing (as the Trinity doctrine also emphasizes). He
chose, however, not to remain the sole reality, but to make
other realities. This is an ethical act. It is analogous to the act
we illustrated by the experiences of Effingham Cooper, Simone
Weil, the Ancient Mariner, and some prisoners of war, in which
the independent reality of others was recognized. God regards
all things with a perfect love, and the experiences we cited are
a way for us to understand the nature of God's perfect love.

We can, however, remain closed and not recognize the independence of others, and instead regard ourselves as unique
centers with all else in orbit around us. But God's situation is
unlike our own. When we do not perceive the reality of others,
they are nonetheless there; but God was in truth the only reality. Our *de facto* uniqueness was inaccurate; but God's *de facto*
uniqueness was accurate. He could have legitimately remained
the only center, the only power around which all that was
himself was related. But he performed an ethical act, not by
recognizing other realities (which he could have done only
were there preexisting matter), but in the first instance by
creating realities when there was nothing. It was an act by
which he limited his power; for the existence of other realities
means he chooses to make and to allow for the existence of

particulars which do not orbit around himself. They are independent foci, which can rightly be objects of interest and concern to one another and to him because, as independent realities, they have legitimate worth.

To have the universe made of preexistent material is to have
stuff which for its existence is not dependent on God's creation;
it is a reality in its own right. This detracts from God's love in
making the universe; for it means he did not go from being the
sole reality to choosing not to be the sole reality. He did not thus
humble himself, because something already existed independently of his will. Creation—which would be the making of
some additional realities from the preexistent material—could
then be only a *recognition* of realities (the preexistent stuff and
what is made of it): this is an act of humility but it is not the same
as an act of humility in which a legitimate uniqueness is relinquished; this kind of creation is not the ethical act of a unique
reality or center of power moving freely from being the only
reality (giving up its uniqueness) for the sake of there being
something besides itself, something that is a reality in its own
right.[3]

In Genesis 1, after the various acts of creation, it is said,
". . . and God saw that it was good." This, on our view of love,
means that it was good that they were there, not because they
were needed by God nor because they were part of himself or
even good because he was their author (though whatever he
makes is good). He saw, recognized, and respected their presence simply because they were what they were. Though they
depend on him utterly, he lets them be there as realities; that
is, as powers and centers. Though they can be bloated ones
when *de facto* centers only, they can as moral centers legitimately be foci in their own right. For these reasons, the creation
doctrine, with its view of God's completeness and his creation
of all things from nothing, is *a* fitting *cosmic* statement of the
kind of love which recognizes the independence of other realities. On the other hand, love as the recognition of the reality of
others, when used to interpret the doctrine as we have done,

enables us to understand that doctrine in a fresh way. It is a doctrine which depicts for us the character or nature of God's love for all things.

The use of preexistent material denies the sovereignty of God, since there is something for whose existence and nature he is not responsible. At one time denial of sovereignty would have been enough to have settled the matter theologically. But why should it make any difference to us now? To have preexistent material denies God's fullness or his completeness. This as we have seen means that he is not the sole reality whose move from this unique position is by the creation of other realities. This seems to me to be a major shortcoming of views of a limited deity, such as we find in Process Theology based on Whitehead's work. In spite of all the claims that such a theology is better able to express a doctrine of love, it fails in this crucial respect to express love as a doctrine of a complete God, who is the sole reality, freely making another reality from nothing.[4] Were God by nature incomplete, instead of enjoying the fullness of the triune life, he could not perform the humble act of limiting himself by the creation of other realities and putting himself in need of them (as we will see shortly). *Such* a love is what a complete God freely creating *ex nihilo* states.[5]

We are here but touching on a vast and difficult topic in philosophical theology which I do not want to go into. I only wish to suggest that behind the Christian doctrine of creation and the problems and bafflement it raises lies the nature of *what* God creates. He created realities; that is, independent particulars which are in no way part of himself, and are in no way able to come into existence without him. The specific formulation given to the Christian doctrine of creation in the early centuries of the Christian era, under pressure from Gnosticism, Neoplatonism, and other philosophical streams, was partly shaped by the need to articulate its view of creation in a fashion that protected its conception of God. But that could be retained only by protecting the reality of *what* God made. When the specific features of the Christian doctrine of creation are seen to retain the reality of particulars, we see that it gives love a cosmic significance. It means that the very existence of the world is a profound act of love; we and all things are at each moment being regarded with a perfect attentiveness, similar to that Effingham Cooper was able to bestow for only a brief moment. We and other particulars exist only because we and they are objects of perfect love. We and they are there only because the only reality there was humbly decided that there should be more than one valuable thing.

I mentioned in the first chapter that it is hard to make room for God in our universe because we cannot conceive of him directly. Here is one way to conceive of him: learn to recognize other realities. You then can conceive of God as one who not only recognizes realities, as you do, but who freely chooses that there should be realities. The more you so love, the more you are overwhelmed by a knowledge of one who perfectly loves, and the more you perceive all things as objects of a perfect love.

This is only a hint of the practical significance of the doctrine, and we will take the matter up more fully in the next chapter. We see, nonetheless, that by integrating the experience of love as found in Effingham Cooper and others with the doctrine of creation, we have a way to form a conception of what the Christian doctrine concretely says and delivers. The doctrine can thus be seen to be more than remote speculation, but part of a framework that articulates the view of love we have discussed with cosmic dimensions. It also gives some reason to hold to a Christian doctrine of creation instead of rival views, such as that of Process Theology, and indeed instead of the present-day view of the world as a self-contained universe. If love matters, this doctrine matters, since it expresses love on a cosmic scale; and love does matter, as we have seen, because to perceive from a moral position is to perceive more realistically.

It should not be utterly surprising that we cannot imagine fully what it is for God to make things from nothing and to sustain them.[6] It is not in our power to make other realities that way: to be the sole reality and to move from this unique position to a shared one. But we can conceive and experience the character of that love. We can do this conceptually by describing, as we have done, in the previous chapter, what it is to recognize perfectly the independence of other things; and we can have that experience to some degree, as we recognize in our perception and action other things as irreducibly particular, worthy of regard for their own sakes.

To study nature as a scientist, if it is done humbly, with the desire to understand it as a focus of value in its own right and not just for its utility, is a religious act. It is to participate (whether knowingly or not) to some degree in the kind of love God bestows on his creation. Putting a child to bed with consideration, or being touched by the beauty of a landscape so that for a moment we lose self-consciousness, is at least to touch the fringe of a love in which the entire universe is perpetually seen by its Maker. The more we are able to recognize other things as irreducible particulars, worthy of regard for their own sakes, and free of our own orbit, the more we can understand God's creation as an act of perfect love, and participate in bestowing that kind of love ourselves.

God's creation as an act of perfect love is affirmed in ontological statements about an *ex nihilo* creation and preservation: acts which are beyond our ability to portray fully,[7] but a doctrine that on a cosmic scale does express the view that the universe is conceived in love and preserved in love. The doctrine thus shows in part how love can be elevated to supreme importance, and we see that the doctrine is more than cosmic speculation about the universe. It affirms that people and things are not only precious to us, but are precious to the Creator of all things.

SECTION II

I have described perfect love as the recognition of the reality of others. This has been done from two standpoints: (1) what it is like to experience the reality of others—using primarily the experience of Effingham Cooper sinking in a bog; (2) what it is like to need to have one's own reality recognized—using the experience of Pattie O'Driscoll. Though we crave to be loved perfectly and to be attached to others, we are incapable of giving such love. According to Murdoch, we may progressively improve in our ability to recognize the reality of others, but for her there is no consummation of love. We never become fully loving nor fully loved; the goal is too distant and the obstacles are too great. And the finality of death nullifies our longing for fulfillment. My conviction, however, is that the situation is changed when love, understood as the self-forgetful awareness of others, is integrated with the Christian doctrines of the Trinity and the kingdom of God. We then have mutual love in its fullness. It is then possible not only for us to progress in our awareness of others but to conceive of a consummation of love. In other words, the moral life—the endeavor to perceive others more accurately—finds its completion in the religious life.

Let us begin with the doctrine of the Trinity. Here we have Father, Son, and Holy Spirit, three persons (or as I shall frequently say, three centers of power). They are irreducible to one another, and yet, they are said to be bound together in such a way as to be a profound unity. How are we to conceive this? Partly, I suggest, in terms of the view of love we developed in the last chapter. On the one hand, love keeps them distinct from one another. For their love is not jealous, with each seeking to take over the other and to reduce the other into orbit around itself. Instead, each recognizes the reality and hence distinctiveness of the other; that very recognition of distinctiveness is love. Yet since love is a bond, that which separates is itself what holds them together.

Yet the relationship cannot be properly stated by the notion of love as far as we have developed it in the previous chapter; for it leaves too great a separation of persons or powers. Their bond of love is not just the mutual recognition of each other's reality. There must also be a mutual giving; and the giving must be such that each possesses the other. The term which best expresses this relation is that of "indwelling." The Father dwells in the Son and the Son dwells in the Father; that is, whatever is the Son's, the Father possesses. It dwells in him by the Son's giving himself over to the Father's power entirely. Likewise, whatever is the Father's dwells in the Son—he possesses it—by the Father's giving himself over to the Son. So too is the Holy Spirit. Thus we find in the Scriptures that when the Father creates all things are made *through* the Son (John 1:3), and all things are made *in* the Son and *for* the Son (Col. 1:16). All things are *permeated* by the Son and made according to his nature (Col. 1:17). Likewise we find that Jesus says of himself: "My food is to do the will of him who sent me, and to accomplish his work" (John 4:34); ". . . I seek not my own will but the will of him who sent me" (John 5:30); "For I have come down from heaven, not to do my own will, but the will of him who sent me" (John 6:38). In Gethsemane he prays that "not my will, but thine, be done" (Luke 22:42); and his devotion to the Father finds its culmination in his obedience "unto death," even a humiliating death on a cross (Phil. 2:5–8).

They dwell fully in one another then, in terms of turning their power over to the others, or in giving themselves freely to the others. They thereby fully possess the others' power. Yet what is the Son, is the Son, though he is present in the Father or is possessed by the Father. What is the Father, is the Father, though he dwells in the Son. Indwelling, then, is a relationship of mutual presence to one another and mutual possession of one another, in such a way as to give unity and oneness and yet to retain distinctiveness. The divine nature, then, is an indwelling of particular centers of power which are united in a relationship of love, because there is a recognition of distinctiveness and yet a mutual giving which is so complete that each power possesses as its own all the power of the others.

This mutual perception and sharing can be imagined in part by an analogy with our mutual perception of one another. We can be not only aware of others, but aware that they are aware of us; and they in turn aware that we are aware that they are aware of us, and so on indefinitely. The regress has in principle no end; we do not know how far in fact we ourselves can go in actual awareness of such mutual awareness. But it may be that perfect awareness of one another (one that involves recognition of the recognition of oneself by another), when it goes far enough, is to give and to possess one another; so that it is to indwell in one another. At any rate, our own experience of mutual perception, though limited, can suggest the excitement, ecstasy, and full absorption of such mutual perception between the Father, Son, and Spirit. It can be used to portray the character of the divine unity as follows.

To indwell in one another is to be so fully aware of the other that there is no self-consciousness; there is an awareness of oneself only insofar as one sees one's effect on the other, but one's concern is for the other. To indwell is to exercise power only on the other's behalf, as one perfectly perceives the other and the effects of one's power. Each in giving himself up actually has at his disposal all the other powers. One power by its exercise, through the sympathetic action of the other powers, exercises all the powers of the Trinity. In the Trinity each power is so thoroughly aware of and concerned for the others that each puts its own power at the others' disposal and each has at its disposal all the power of the others. The result is a unity in power; yet because it is based upon a mutual awareness, there are distinct centers of power.

As we pointed out a moment ago, God can create freely and *ex nihilo* because he is complete. But his completeness should not suggest stillness. Because God is a Trinity, the divine life is dynamic: it is a mutual giving and possessing that is an eternal (in the sense of continuous) giving and possessing. There is among the centers of power a continuous and continuing perception of one another and a continuous giving and receiving of one another. Life there is abundant. He is the living God.

The idea of endless repetition may seem utterly boring to us; we seem to need variety. Perhaps this playful passage from G. K. Chesterton can suggest to us how repetition may spring from vitality.

A man varies his movements because of some slight element of failure or fatigue. He gets into an omnibus because he is tired of walking; or he walks because he is tired of sitting still. But if his life and joy were so gigantic that he never tired of going to Islington, he might go to Islington as regularly as the Thames goes to Sheerness. The very speed and ecstacy of his life would have the stillness of death. The sun rises every morning. I do not rise every morning; but the variation is due not to my activity, but to my inaction. Now, to put the matter in a popular phrase, it might be true that the sun rises regularly because he never gets tired of rising. His routine might be due, not to a lifelessness, but to a rush of life. The thing I mean can be seen, for instance, in children, when they find some game or joke that they specially enjoy. A child kicks his legs rhythmically through excess, not absence, of life. Because children have abounding vitality, because they are in spirit fierce and free, therefore they want things repeated and unchanged. They always say, "Do it again"; and the grown-up person does it again until he is nearly dead. For grown-up people are not strong enough to exult in monotony. But perhaps God is strong enough to exult in monotony. It is possible that God says every morning, "Do it again" to the sun; and every evening, "Do it again" to the moon.[8]

Maybe this is why there is so much empty space in our universe; God does not find it monotonous.

The doctrine of the Trinity is distinctive to Christianity, and it is greatly responsible for the distinctiveness of the Christian view of love. We are not only created particulars, respected as centers of reality, but it is our destiny to move toward participation in the divine life and hence to a consummation of love; for the triune God has freely granted men the opportunity to participate in his inner life. We are to come to recognize that we are each different realities, and yet to seek to attain an indwelling, one within the other.

The life of the Trinity is a perfect community and it is the kind of community for which we long; for it satisfies our craving to be loved perfectly and to be attached to others properly. In giving ourselves to others by a perfect regard for them, we find that they perfectly love us, and so we retain our distinctiveness.

It is a unity in which we continue to be, and yet one in which we are fully possessed and fully possess. The Trinity—the true community—cannot be achieved here and now, but it is the life we crave and which even now we can begin to enter to the extent to which we improve in our recognition of each other's reality. We are creatures, however, and remain creatures; that is, realities which are legitimate foci of interest, concern, and worth but nonetheless ones which have been made and which remain reality only by the divine creativity. Our indwelling in God, his in us, and ours in each other, whereby each perceives the others as they are and each puts the riches of himself at the disposal of the others, is not the Trinity but the kingdom of God. It is the divine Trinity *and* human creatures (and perhaps more as well), indwelling in one another. We perceive and enjoy the reality of each other, giving and receiving. We do not seek to retain our *de facto* reality, but lose self-consciousness in our absorption by the reality of others. We perceive our own worth indirectly by noticing our effect on others whom we now perceive regarding us lovingly as we lovingly regard them. So even though this is not the Trinity but the kingdom of God, it is held together by the same kind of love that unites the powers that are God into unity, and bind us all into a unity where there is diversity, where there is God and his creatures.

This is the doctrine of our divinization. As taught over the centuries by the Eastern Orthodox churches, it is not that we become God, but that we take part in the life of God by sharing in the kind of indwelling found there between distinct powers. By having that kind of relationship between ourselves, one with the other, and with God, we take part in the life of God.

We can now see how the framework of Christian doctrines, when integrated with the view of love as the recognition of other realities, is enriched and itself enriches and subtly alters the character of love. For the breathtaking and outlandish wonder of the Christian vision is that God, who is complete and rich in his own triune life, humbles himself by making other realities, so that he is not the sole reality. God's love is not a mere recognition of realities, which is itself a profound act of love, but also the creation of other realities. Second, he humbles himself in that the goal of the universe is that he share his life with us, and we in him share our lives with each other. That is to say, he now *needs* us in order for there to be a kingdom of God. The kingdom is not just each of us finding fulfillment in God—he alone does not satisfy; part of the kingdom is our participation in each other. This is needed for our fulfillment as well. And our indwelling in each other is an indwelling in which he too will share. He neither needed to make realities nor to give them and himself a destiny to dwell in one another; for he had a complete and full life in himself without any other reality but his own. But by so doing, he *now* has a dependence on us for the consummation of creation and for his own satisfaction, one freely undertaken and because freely undertaken more profoundly humble and loving.[9]

The second Genesis account of creation graphically illustrates our point. In that story, Adam is put in paradise, with a glorious garden, with animals to interest him, and with the presence of God himself to enjoy. Yet Adam is lonely; something is missing; he lacks what can give completeness. Even with the unique reality, the Fountain of realities, God himself, Adam needs something else. God perceives this, and is not jealous, but graciously creates a woman for him. What he needs for his own completeness and satisfaction is another like himself. She is made from his own flesh (not from dust as he was). Yet she is not completely like him: her sexual difference alone is not what makes her of interest, but being like and yet different from him, there can be a mutual enrichment in a mutual perception and giving. This illustrates that our fulfillment involves not only a right relationship with God but a mutual giving and receiving of one another as well, a fulfillment God recognizes and endorses.[10]

SECTION III

Now as I have said, we crave to be loved and need to be loved; we are promised in the Trinity a consummation of love.

But suffering and death are necessary for the consummation of love. For love within the Trinity is a suffering and painful love. The Son, who became incarnate, was crucified. That suffering Lord is present in the heart of the divine; the suffering of the Son indwells in the Father and Holy Spirit.

What this means is that God chose by creation to make realities—true powers—to be and to be perceived as centers of existence, and he made them to love and to be loved, specifically for an indwelling love, like his own. But as we saw in the last chapter, especially in the novel about Pattie O'Driscoll, to be a reality is to be a *de facto* person. It involves perceiving other realities in orbit around oneself; and their very reality is a threat to us, for they threaten to break down our own centrality, and to reveal the unreality of the position we occupy. So each of us regards the other from a *de facto* stance and is regarded from that stance. This means we outrage each other's true worth, and each of us resists such an outrage. Our rightful desire to be recognized as a particular with true worth is overlaid with an unrealistic *de facto* worth, and our true worth is not perceived by others or by ourselves.

It is well to ask ourselves: was it hard for God to create the universe? It is not a question of the need to exercise great force to make such a vast universe; instead it is the necessity of withdrawing himself so that we might exist as centers of reality in our own right, and the need for him to endure the outrages we perform against each other.

So for the kind of love that is in God to be among men, suffering on his part and on our part is necessary. He respects us as centers of power, so that he does not interfere with our lives in such a way as to force us to recognize the reality of other things. We must attain that perception ourselves. He suffers because of this. For he perceives the suffering in all things; he is aware of the vulnerability and hunger to be loved that is there. He regards us with the enormous pity that Christ exhibited on the cross: "Father, forgive them; for they know not what they do." He makes provision for our attainment of moral perception for ourselves: the very existence of others and the mutual need of creatures for each other, and awareness of the power to injure and destroy one another, is one way we can be moved from a *de facto* position. The love of parents, even when little more perhaps than animal warmth (as we saw with Pattie's mother), is a partial recognition and stirring of our own irreducible particularity; the responsibilities of social living and even the process of socialization[11] in growing up are ways one learns what it is to live with and to recognize the reality of others.

Yet we are *de facto* persons; isolated one from the other (and from God) by the profound unreality of the unbounded horizon that is ourself. Each of us is like a field of force, attracting all things around us, and at the same time repelling their reality. He made us that way: as powers, to be related to himself by a voluntary self-giving recognition on our part of each other and of him. It is the very greatness of our destiny, of our power to indwell in one another by our own self-giving and humble reception, that opens us and God to enormous suffering. The height to which we may rise is a good indication of the depths to which we may fall. He loves enough that we should be foci of independent and legitimate value. Yet because he loves as Son and Spirit, we are called out of isolation; and that process of coming out of isolation is the process of life as we know it: involving profound suffering, misunderstanding, loneliness, hatred, manipulation, fantastic self-aggrandizement, and a countless multitude of less than perfect loves. The search for indwelling love is thus destructive but the source of unimaginable fulfillment.

The kingdom of God is to be created in part by us, and without any blueprint; for we are powers and what that indwelling is to be depends on what we are able to create in ourselves and among ourselves as our contribution to the mutual life in the kingdom. What is to come, we are partly bringing, and it does not yet exist. Nonetheless, as Paul said, faith and hope pass away; only love endures forever. We have, then, some idea of the kingdom to come, since we can know something of love here and now. But we do not presently perceive each other so as to indwell. We love and perceive so badly that we do not experience the profound sharing that allows both unity and diversity. Therefore we do not understand God very well, since he is unity with diversity—a Trinity; nor do we understand ourselves very well, since our destiny and goal is to move toward the kingdom of God, where what we truly are will be finally revealed. ". . . I shall understand fully, even as I have been fully understood." (1 Cor. 13:12)

There is, then, an enormous gap or chasm between what we are as *de facto* persons, and the indwelling love of the Trinity. There is no way to bridge that gap, there is no way to leap over it; we cannot get to an indwelling love in one determined resolve. For the goal is not only to love God, but to get ourselves into a right relation to all realities. We cannot leap outside the social relations we have with others. Our families, our town, our country, our time cannot be left behind. The particulars he has created, and the particular social contexts in which we find ourselves, are the places where we are to refine our perceptions of reality—to learn what is there, to learn to improve our relations to it, and to love it. It is here that our *de facto* perceptions are to be shed. This world and the next, then, are not the same, but the connection between them is *the movement toward an indwelling love through a more realistic perception of this world*. We will never attain a proper relation to all realities in this life. The attainment of an indwelling love then requires a life beyond death, and the transformation of our bodies and material universe. But an indwelling love is not pie in the sky; for it is a life vitally connected to our present one and present world. The struggle to attain realistic perceptions and rightly ordered relations is the concern of this life, and an indwelling love is the consummation of this life.

We have now given a framework for the experience of love which Murdoch presents. The framework elevates love to a place of supremacy both in an ontological sense by the creation doctrine (the very existence of the universe is an act of love), and in a historical sense by a movement through time that is intrinsically connected to a goal beyond history. And it is a framework which affects the very character of that love by its view of creation *ex nihilo* and by its inclusion of a consummation.

The content of these doctrines is by no means exhausted by the approach we have employed. They have been treated primarily to develop a view of love. This has enabled us to see these doctrines as related very closely indeed to our human condition, even though they are also highly speculative cosmic doctrines. But in a universe open apparently to so many possible ways of being understood, this view of love provides a reason to consider the interpretation of the universe under God as a plausible and attractive one, and this view of love can be used as one standard in the evaluation of other theological interpretations. This we have illustrated by some negative remarks about Process Theology, whereby we showed that its view of a limited God did not allow a statement of God's love as one which freely creates and freely becomes dependent on us and which promises us a consummation of our longing to be rightly loved.

Our individual religious life is not uniform in strength all of the time. There are moments of intense spiritual awareness when we are very receptive to Christian truths. There are also long periods of time, lasting perhaps months or even years, in which we are on a plateau. Words and thoughts which once meant a great deal to us now fail to inspire us, and new ideas do not easily gain an entrance into our minds and hearts. A great deal, then, depends on the rhythms of the spiritual life, as we move in and out of the shadows.

People also have different ways of expressing their ideas, and sometimes it is only after considerable discussion and much give-and-take that they realize how deep their agreement is and how apparently alien ideas are really quite compatible with their own.

It may be useful, too, to bear in mind the distinction between the order of knowing and the order of being; that is, the order in which one finds out things and the order in which they stand. One might, for example, learn in ballet how to walk, do demi-pliés, and then to pirouette—in that order; but in no actual ballet that one dances, do they stand in that order. The Trinity is not where one begins to learn about God; most of us who are believers did not begin there. Israel did not know of a Son, even though there are interesting hints of some distinctions within God in the Old Testament. So it is to be expected that one should find talk of a triune love unacceptable or at least remote from the struggles of our daily life. But it seems to me that we, who cannot apparently work with many of the ontological categories of the early Christian centuries, or of the Middle Ages, or with those now proffered by Whiteheadians, can by use of the experience of love, and ethical portrayals of love, reinterpret the old doctrines. We can then start to see in them something we had perhaps not seen before, to sense that the gospel is more than we had realized, and to begin once again to perceive its riches and relevance. And perhaps above all, we can get an enriched vision about what we are called upon to do in our daily life (a matter I will turn to in the next chapter).

Our situation today is rather like that of the Russian exile in *The Time of the Angels.* Out of the wreck of his past, he possessed only a shred: an icon of the blessed Trinity. He did not know what to make of it. We live in the aftermath of a debacle of a culture and a church which offers only a shred of life-giving truth. We are a wreck (albeit an interesting, fascinating, even glorious wreck), but not a total one. We do have something— a tremendous religious heritage; our task is to re-possess what we have that we may live—not each one unto himself—but in each other and in the truth. Our task is to get into a position to perceive what is there, a task for both the heart and mind.

Chapter Four

WHAT MUST BE DONE:
A Profile of the Contemporary Christian

*

C. S. Lewis once wrote that he abandoned philosophical Idealism and became a Christian precisely because, in contrast to that philosophical school, Christianity was primarily something to be done. I have given an interpretation of some major Christian doctrines which taken together amount to a high-theological understanding of the universe. The question now is, What are we to do? What according to this theology is the profile, so to speak, of the spiritual person?

The first thing one is supposed to do is to pay attention. This is a most demanding action. It can be performed only as one gains some freedom from the competing desires which pull us in diverse directions, but which all conspire to feed our inordinate desire for significance, so that we cannot attend properly to what is before us. We are continually to remind ourselves of this fact, and to relook at incidents that have occurred—such as when a child asked us to play with him, or when we were confronted by an angry customer, or when we became ill. We are to reexamine our reactions so as to increase our awareness of the way our estimate of what occurred was colored by our tendency to perceive everything as though it were in orbit around ourselves. My anger, for example, at the failure of my students to understand a difficult problem may upon reflection be seen to result from an uneasiness about my teaching ability. This anger and uneasiness prevents me from realizing how hard they are trying and how insecure they are about their ability to learn. We can thus increasingly learn what it is that limits our ability to attend to others and hence to respond in a way that is more fitting to the particular realities we encounter.

However much people may be like each other, and despite the fact that there are billions of people, each person rightly craves to be recognized as an irreducible center of worth. But we often overlook the significance of the particular in favor of the general. This can be illustrated by the way those in positions of management—whether in church work, education, business, or medicine—are usually regarded as far more significant than those who work on the ground floor where one is face to face with the individuals who are being catered for. A seminary professor is surrounded by more glory than most parish ministers. A research doctor in a medical center has more prestige than most practitioners. Yet knowledge that is in a great theological or medical center is of no use unless it is taken to individuals who are in need. Those at a center exist largely as auxiliaries to the practitioner, to help supply him with what is needed. Yet almost everyone nowadays aspires to be at the center, for that is where the glory is. But attention needs to be directed to where there are people in need. One need not feel inferior because he is away from a center. Every place where there are people is a place that matters, for particulars have an irreplaceable worth.

The importance of attention to particular realities can also be illustrated by the fact of death. Every person must die, and because this is so, most of life goes on without much notice of the vast majority of deaths. Death (as we will show later) is sociologically marginal today. Yet the task of attending to a person at the last is a moral and a religious task; it is to recognize and to respect that person's particularity. Much of one's Christian life is socially unimportant because it consists of paying attention to individual people in a universe where there are so many people that only a few of them rate general notice. Yet Jesus thought that holding children on his knee was part of the kingdom of God.

Social situations or relations are not, however, insignificant. They are to be seen in terms of their own individuality as well. There are many general truths about family life, but they should not become a barrier to our recognition that each family is also a particular family with its own distinctiveness. It may take great care and attentiveness to understand a particular family and its own dynamics. We have then to pay attention especially to our own family and to come to terms with its distinctive reality.

In the same fashion, each of us lives in a country, a particular country, with its own heritage, its own demands and obligations, its own failings and glories. Jesus knew what it was to live in a conquered country, and what it was like to be a tax collector, a fisherman, or a Pharisee. He related to those particulars according to their own reality, with a freedom that often broke through the stereotyped estimates of these people, so that his reception of some and his castigation of others was quite surprising. So too are we to attend to our own country, to its system of laws, its economic system, its social groups, its history, and its foreign relations. We are to seek to overcome our ignorance, our self-interest, our prejudices, so that we can see more accurately the reality that is there and thereby respond to it more adequately.

According to the religious world view we have presented, our study of the workings of nature (as we briefly mentioned earlier) is a God-given task. Scientific investigation deals with realities which as such are worthy of attention and understanding. The universe is not a stage for a drama of salvation to be played out, as it has so often been portrayed in theology, but our very investigation of nature—the desire to see it as it really is —is a moral and religious task. The study of nature is not an extra tacked onto the real business of being religious; it is integral to the religious task. We are to seek to perceive clearly the realities of the natural world. Our very moral growth, our sanctification, takes place in this endeavor.

This view is not the same as Tillich's, in which all activities are part of the search for the Ground of Being, as though they were stepping-stones or substitutes for the real object of our search, viz., God. Rather, this view calls for a wholehearted attentive search for the reality of what is before one. Though it indeed depends on God for its reality, its reality is irreducible to another reality even if that reality be God's. He made it from nothing to be a reality independent of his own reality. Hence the ability to study and understand the natural world with brilliant success apart from direct reference to the reality of God is consistent with the moral and religious view that there is a respect for the particularity of each item by God. So scientists, and all those engaged in all academic disciplines, are engaged in a religious pursuit to the extent that they are motivated by the desire to perceive more accurately the reality which surrounds us and of which we are a part.

Such attention need not be restricted to professionals. A respect for living creatures of all kinds, and even of inanimate things, can be shown by a recognition of their independent reality. The sheer beauty of the universe, both to the intellect as it penetrates into its workings and its appearance to the senses, can evoke a wonder and a respect which oblige us to temper the way we think and act. Plato taught that beauty is a gateway to goodness; that is, beauty by its appeal to our senses and intellect has the ability to arrest our attention and momentarily break our self-attentive *de facto* stance. If we then seize the opportunity created by the recognition of beauty, we can steadily train ourselves to move away from a *de facto* stance in relation to all things, even when we are not at that moment aware of their beauty. In this time of ecological crisis, such attentiveness is exceedingly relevant; for we have been so mesmerized by the glory and grandeur of wealth that we have been unable to regard the earth as a reality which has, merely as a reality, some independence of our wants and desires and hence is worthy of respect. Our self-centered, solipsistic relation to nature now promises to reap what it has sown.

We conclude our first point that one of our tasks is to pay attention by a quotation from G. K. Chesterton.

> No two ideals could be more opposite than a Christian saint in a Gothic cathedral and a Buddhist saint in a Chinese temple. The opposition exists at every point; but perhaps the shortest statement of it is that the Buddhist saint always has his eyes shut, while the Christian saint always has them very wide open. The Buddhist saint has a sleek and harmonious body, but his eyes are heavy and sealed with sleep. The mediaeval saint's body is wasted to its crazy bones, but his eyes are frightfully alive. . . . Granted that both images are extravagances, . . . it must be a real divergence which could produce such opposite extravagances. The Buddhist is looking with a peculiar intentness inwards. The Christian is staring with a frantic intentness outwards.[1]

What is taking place in time and space in the world about us must be attended to; it is here, in an attentiveness that breaks the illusion of our self-centered fantasy world made up of our false self-importance, that the kingdom of God begins to dawn. The reality of the world begins to emerge as we ourselves begin to experience ourselves as but one reality among many. Then its goodness, its fascinating splendor, begins to reveal itself. It is seen as the object of a perfect love—God's.

This brings us to the second thing that is to be done. We are to learn to see ourselves as an object of a perfect love. We illustrated the idea of perfect love by the experience of Effingham Cooper sinking in a bog, and by J. R. Jones' account of Coleridge's Ancient Mariner. These illustrations gave us a glimpse of how God himself regards his creatures: looking on what he called out of nothing with a profound and never ceasing attentiveness.

The religious or spiritual person has moved sufficiently on occasions from the bonds of his blinding *de facto* perspective to have a glimpse of what is meant by perfect love. But this sets a task for him: to learn how to combine in a single consciousness the fact that he is but one item among billions upon billions of realities and yet simultaneously the apple of the Lord's eye. To learn how to see himself as an object of a perfect love is to learn to combine in a single moment of consciousness the fact that he is but dust and ashes and yet a little lower than the angels, an animal and yet bearing the image of God. It is to be humble and yet to be aware of one's imperishable worth.

A marvelous example of what we are to seek to realize can be found in Luke 1:46–55, where Mary, the mother of Jesus, sings a song to magnify what God has done in selecting her to bear the Christ. In that song we see that Mary realized that Christ's coming to a lowly maiden meant that the proud had been passed over. She saw that the mighty had been put down from their thrones, and those of low degree exalted. She saw that the hungry are to be filled with good things; the rich are to be sent away empty-handed. In other words, Mary understood the gospel, perceived immediately what it meant. She understood what her elevation meant. Yet Mary, who was elevated, remained humble. She who is honored above all women did not become proud. She is known to the disciples and the early Christian believers as one who bore the Christ Child but who remained humble. This is why she is to be honored; she is the great example for us to follow. She shows us how we are to receive Christ. For we too are elevated by God; we creatures made from nothing are called to be sons of the Most High, to dwell on high with him forever and ever. And yet like Mary we are to remain humble. As she performs her mundane tasks of childbearing and child-rearing, cooking and sewing, so too are we to engage ourselves in the ordinary tasks of life.

This brings us to the third thing we are to do. We are not to seek to live in glory before our time. The experience of perfect love that was illustrated by Effingham Cooper's adventure is so beautiful and appealing that we may become impatient with our present condition. The goal of the consummation of love is so compelling and our craving need to be loved is so great that we are tempted to "leap" to it, or to think that we can, if we just try hard enough, attain such perfection in this life. But we forget the enormous depths of sin, the frightful power of that boundless horizon that is ourselves. The height to which we may ascend is a good measure of the depth to which we may descend, and that deep pit must be completely filled and cease to exercise its influence before we can live in the glory of a mutual, indwelling love.

It is possible for people by chance to have the experience of perfect love, as we saw in the case of Cooper. A conjunction of circumstances may come together so that for a moment our *de facto* person is inoperative. But this is only momentary, and though it can have lasting good effects, it can also amount to nothing, as in the case of Cooper.

So we are not to strive to leap over what we are and get to the goal of perfect love in a single bound. Rather, we are to come to terms with the knowledge that we are *de facto* persons and that we are going to remain such throughout this life. Even a saint does not remain in a perpetual state of love. He feels the pressure of other people and powers on himself, and the bodily and psychic forces of which he is not fully in control, that draw him back into the position where all is seen from the perspective of his self at the center.

It is terribly dangerous to think that one can attain perfection in this life. We saw in the case of the heroine of *The Unicorn* that willful withdrawal of oneself into passivity was not only impossible but that it led to a self-deception that ultimately resulted in the destruction of herself and many others around her. Self-deception not only leads to the denial of the forces within oneself, and a misinterpretation of one's actions and motives, it also keeps one from recognizing the nature of God's love for us. For it is a *de facto* person he loves; that person who magnifies his own worth is graciously pitied and regarded with compassion. To live a life that denies the reality of oneself is to live without the experience of the graciousness of God's love.

The desire to leap beyond the reality of our present condition also encourages self-righteousness and hatred. For our evil is often projected onto others. It is true that others are indeed full of evil, so we can almost always find some justification for what we say. But at the same time our own evil is not removed. It becomes uglier, and damaging to us, because unadmitted and unperceived, and we become merciless in our criticism of others.

The desire to live in glory before our time also opens us up to Utopian illusions. Reinhold Niebuhr was a great revealer of this tendency in American and Western culture. He traced the recurrent appeal of Utopianism to a neglect of the reality of sin and its ineradicable nature. One of the many ingredients in the social upheavals in the student movements of the 1960's seems to have been Utopian idealism. On the other hand, those comfortably placed can use the inaccessibility of Utopian solutions as a way to avoid all criticism of the *status quo* and possible improvements.

Perhaps one other manifestation of the desire to live in glory before our time is the present emphasis on mind-expansion or consciousness-expansion. Some of its exponents are from the East, and though variously related to Eastern religions, they have dropped much of their own Eastern theology when they teach in America. Although they emphasize different things, nearly all of them seek to help one achieve an expanded awareness. I am sympathetic with at least that tiny fraction of this phenomena of which I have some knowledge; for I interpret it to contain within it a desire to help people escape from the bondage of *de facto* lives and from the dissatisfaction, even misery, felt by many. I am also sympathetic because the theology of perfect love I have presented stresses the need for a new awareness and a new perception of ourselves, our universe, and God. But the theology of perfect love emphasizes that such awareness is beyond our present life. We can progressively improve in this life; perhaps attain it momentarily. But the way we are to live and to engage ourselves is by attentiveness to particulars—particular persons, situations, and tasks. We are to seek to be more adequately related to others, not to seek a particular state of consciousness to enjoy. Many acts of love are not fun, as a careful reconsideration of some of the examples we have given in this book will make evident.

The fourth thing a religious person does is to pay attention to Jesus and to confess what he sees there. In terms of the ideas we have developed, this means that people who occupy a *de facto* position—unable to perceive other realities—also do not perceive the reality of Jesus. Even if a person sometimes perceives the reality of others, he may still never in the various presentations of Jesus in books, stories, songs, and sacraments break from a *de facto* self-concern and perceive him as an independent reality. But if we are able to see him as a particular, that is, break through our self-concern and prejudices about him, then we find ourselves up against someone who pays attention to us. His entire life is portrayed as a reaction to what he sees in us. His very coming, his every deed, is a response to what he perceives about us. So if we pay attention to him, we can see what we are, for all that he does is a reaction to us.[2]

What then do we see when we pay attention to him? We perceive that our person causes him suffering. He suffers because of the suffering we cause each other. The truth about ourselves is not only that we as particulars are vulnerable, longing to be loved as particulars, aspiring greatly, and full of *de facto* self-concern, but we are causes of immense, unmerited, and innocent suffering. My consumption of resources is well out of proportion to the available supply for mankind, yet I rarely give serious attention to the suffering of those I have never seen, even though I know in theory that their suffering is as real as any I have ever had.

But in Jesus we perceive that our person as a source of suffering is forgiven, not punished. By his response to us, we perceive what we are: each of us is a particular reality that is loved, accepted, and forgiven, the very particular whose person is a source of immense and unmerited suffering. We may also see ourselves in his resurrection. Our effect on him is that he must die and be transformed; that is his response to us. In this response we may perceive that the person we are must die so as to be transformed and to find a consummation—that we are loved with that sort of love. His entire life, then, is a response to us. By his undeviating attention to us and by his response to what he perceives, we may perceive what our person does to him and thereby what we are.

A person may be aware that he causes immense innocent and unmerited suffering apart from Jesus, and he likewise may be aware of some degree of forgiveness, even perhaps complete release from guilt, or at least be able to live with his guilt. But what one perceives of oneself in Jesus is affected by who Jesus is seen to be. We see ourselves in him only because, and only when, we see him as a perfect lover. That is, he is the one who perceives with undivided attention. Only so is he seen to be the one who suffers for the particular person that I am, who forgives that particular person, dies for the transformation of that life and seeks to indwell with it. I see myself as an object of a perfect love because I see him as a perfect lover. I cannot see myself in Jesus, as the one to whom he responds, unless I see him as God incarnate; for God is a perfect lover, the one who perceives with undivided attention.[3] To perceive Jesus as the one who perceives us with undivided attention because his entire life is a response to our particularity is indirectly to perceive the power and presence of the invisible and incorporeal God. It is to perceive a power of the Trinity incarnate, come to give us the divine life.

The final thing we must do is to forsake the world. This phrase is hardly a popular one today. It is rather scandalous to suggest that we need to forsake the world. We have been told recently on all sides that we need to put our hands to the task of righting injustice, removing oppression and soul-destroying poverty, and to resist the evils of technology. And indeed we do; most emphatically we do. But to forsake the world is not to reject the world. To forsake the world is to realize that there is nothing you know of, have experienced, or can imagine, which would satisfy you.

This attitude is perfectly compatible with a recognition of the glories of the world, its radiant beauty, its delights, its satisfactions, its wonders, and all the rest. It is not a realization which comes because you are a failure, or depressed, or live perhaps in a time of historical decline, or because you are temperamentally a pessimist. However optimistic one is about life on earth, however one conceives of what it can give in the way of pleasure, fame, justice, or goodness, one's heart can long and thirst for something more—something undefined, unknown, unnamed. There is just an emptiness—an emptiness that can exist alongside the fullest, most active life imaginable.

This sense of forsaking the world—a sense of emptiness or of a void to be filled—should not be dismissed as a passing mood. Moods are rather like a weather front moving in; they eclipse everything else, pervade us completely for a time, and then pass away. Forsaking the world is not a mood. It is important to stress this because we all know the mood in which everything tastes like dust and ashes, or as we say, we have the blues. Because we sometimes have such a mood, we can misidentify forsaking the world with such a mood, something we are to shake off and forget, as one of those things which come over people but which are not to be taken too seriously. Instead of this, forsaking the world is an attitude. That is, it can exist alongside laughter, hearty fun, delight in a child, a full and active life. It does not drive everything else out, as does a mood. It does not rob things of value.

Now if this recognition that there is nothing which does satisfy one fully is held onto and not dismissed or ignored as just an unusual sort of quirk, then one is in a condition in which he can receive God's presence. The reception of God's presence takes place when a person by exposure to the Christian religion begins to find that his emptiness is touched and the void in him partly assuaged. One is by no means fully satisfied, but one is getting nourishment, getting the *kind* of satisfaction which nothing else gives. An incident of Jesus' life, one of his parables, a hymn, a celebration of a sacrament, the Lord's Prayer, even the very thought that there is one who cares, helps fill that void. It is this feeding which gives a person the assurance that what is being talked about in a religion is true; it is this contact with something different from all earthly realities that enables faith to arise. One is met by a presence which cannot be seen but which is known when one forsakes the world and finds a distinctive and unique longing being satisfied.[4]

To one who has forsaken the world and who finds himself being spiritually nourished, the entire surrounding environment is seen to be dependent on another reality. One does not perceive the universe as a self-contained and complete reality. One's own longing for what it cannot provide enables one to recognize its incompleteness. He now lives, moves, and breathes in, touches and knocks against a tangible, visible universe which he perceives to be dependent on another reality. That reality is not directly perceived, but insofar as what is seen and handled is seen to be incomplete, another reality is perceived indirectly.

The existence, immensity, and magnificent order of the universe is now perceived as the exhibition of the power and wisdom of God. It is *his* power and *his* wisdom that are seen exhibited in another reality, in its very existence and order. A person can therefore enjoy learning more and more about the workings of all things in the universe, their variety, history, and immensity; he can enjoy them for their own glorious reality, and for their manifestation of the power and wisdom of God.

In short we can say that much of the task of a Christian is the task of actually perceiving what is there to be perceived. There is indeed room for God in the universe, despite the recent panic in theology. But one must get into a position to perceive his presence. That requires attentiveness, humility, and a longing for what the world cannot provide.

Chapter Five

THE MEANING OF DEATH

*

We have argued that most of the time we see things solely from our point of view. Even when we have made some progress toward the genuine recognition of others, the goal toward which we are to move is still far distant. When we now ask, How successful can we expect people to be? there seems to be only one possible answer. Our achievement of a mutual recognition, so that a profound unity of mutual giving and receiving emerges, does not seem possible. Death comes before we achieve perfect love; the progress we have made toward the goal is wiped out.

Not only do we have to face this lack of completion, but death is itself a serious barrier to faith in the reality of God's love for us. We sometimes have literally before us, as in the case of the child in the hospital, with whose story we began, a lifeless body. For those who lose a loved one, the reality of death is a concrete fact; the hope of a life beyond the grave is a hope which needs very persuasive support indeed to be sustained.

Closely connected with the challenge to faith which we face with death is the way things often do not go right for most of us in our daily lives. We suffer losses in our business, our children do poorly in school, we suffer terribly from illnesses, we have accidents and know many disappointments. Are we indeed children of a loving Father? If we were more fully committed to him and prayed more faithfully to him, would he indeed protect us from all these things and grant us more successful lives?

We will deal with these questions in the remainder of this book, showing in this chapter how death is to be regarded by a person who has begun to move out of the enclosed perspective of his own personal point of view and begun to experience the reality of others. Then in the next chapter we will describe the grounds for our hope in the resurrection of the dead and the transformation of ourselves and the entire universe. Finally in the last chapter we will consider the fact that much in life is disappointing and ask what it is that we are to expect from God in this life. The entire discussion is undergirded by a disciplined conception of the religious life. Just as we have seen in the previous chapters that a sustained moral effort is necessary for us to lose our "ontological uniqueness" and to see ourselves as but one reality among many, so too in what follows the same rigorous deflation of our self-importance is called for.

Only in this way can we escape from the charge that the Christian belief in an afterlife is based on the desire for consolation. For it is frequently said that we are to face the suffering of mankind, men's failure to love and to be loved, and their extinction by death, without the consolation of a world to come. Murdoch herself suggests that to hope for a consummation of love is to be unrealistic, and hence immoral, for it is to protect oneself from perceiving the pointlessness of the universe.[1]

It seems to me that this moral objection to a consummation is correct only if indeed there is no God. Should one have good grounds to believe that there is a Christian God, then one is not being unrealistic and thereby immoral to believe in the consummation of love. Still, there is some justification for Murdoch's objection to the idea of a life beyond death, because there is no doubt that many people who believe in life after death do so at least in part out of a fear of death. This probably has contributed to the hesitation to affirm a life beyond death by some contemporary theologians (Bultmann, H.R. Niebuhr, Ogden, Cobb), and to its outright rejection by at least one (Hartshorne). Life after death is also often used as an incentive to moral behavior. One is to do good not because it is good but to get to heaven and to avoid hell. So at this point we will consider the meaning of death and the Christian doctrine of an afterlife. A deeper understanding of the Christian view of eternal life will dispel these charges. After we have considered all of the matters we have mentioned which are associated with the meaning of death, we will turn to the grounds for our hope in the resurrection of the dead.

Section I

It has been said that sex used to be the forbidden subject but that now it is death about which there is silence. Even with its respectability as a philosophical topic in Germany, thanks to Heidegger, and a recent flood of books,[2] it is still worth pointing out the infrequency of its discussion, even by those in medicine and in the ministry who, of all people, encounter it frequently.

Consider, for example, these findings. In a study of a retirement community in California, we find that 80 percent of those surveyed (who ranged in age from fifty to eighty-six) would want their doctor to tell them if they suffered from an incurable disease and death was imminent. But about 75 percent of the respondents have never discussed the subject of dying with either their physician or their clergyman. Other studies reveal that 96 percent of doctors either customarily do not tell—or do not want to tell—patients when death is imminent.[3] A professor of mental health, W. A. Cramond of Adelaide University in Australia reports in an article in the *British Medical Journal* that 80 percent of dying patients know they are nearing death and yearn to talk about it, but 80 percent of the physicians believe that terminal patients should not be told of their condition. He claims that standard textbooks for medical and nursing students make no mention of attitudes toward the dying, and he urges special training for them, hospital social workers and chaplains to deal with the emotional needs of the dying patient.[4]

These findings are but a fragment of the accumulating data which indicate a massive denial of death in present-day Western industrial societies. Apparently one reason for the increase in literature on death is the desire to gain more enlightened humanitarian treatment for the dying, especially in such matters as the efforts to obtain their complicity in denying their own death.[5] Our concern here, however, is not with the problems connected with dying, but with what death means. Once we have shown the difficulty in answering that question, we will have set the stage for a theological appraisal of death, and for a reply to the moral objections to an afterlife.

Consider the view that death is a natural function of the cyclical process of nature. There is a regular cycle of birth, maturation, aging, and finally dissolution. Here the stress is on the commonness of death, its naturalness, and its prosaic insignificance. As Stegmüller puts it,

> Only an egocentric, self-important man sees something alarming and terrifying in dread and death. But from a cosmic point of view, the death of an individual appears as an insignificant episode in the total stream of world events. It is the unnatural bent for prolonged self-examination that is responsible for the artificially induced dread of death, which thereafter seems to take on metaphysical importance.[6]

From one perspective no doubt death is a cosmically insignificant business. But we immediately recognize that this is not all that there is to it. First, human beings are conscious of the fact that one day they will die. Second, prior to all theoretical and academic reflection, people are concerned with themselves. It is not just "an egocentric self-important man" but all of us who have a concern with ourselves that envelops us, a concern we do not have for anyone or anything else, and one which none of us can fully shake off, at least in this life. These two facts utterly transform the question, What is death? It is not merely the prosaic insignificant passing away of something, for we are on one occasion uniquely involved with what is to pass away.

Not only do we know about death and care about it, but we adopt an attitude towards it. Since our attitude is affected by the beliefs we hold, what death means can take a myriad of forms. Christianity, Communism, Positivism, and Platonism have different views about what the nature of reality is, and each accordingly regards death differently. But let me illustrate how the meaning of death is affected not only by beliefs about reality but by the social setting in which it occurs by a summary of some material gathered by R. L. Staples.[7]

He points out that the impact of death depends on many factors and their interplay which no one has yet fathomed. Some obvious factors, however, can be illustrated by a few demographic statistics on death in the U.S. and the Cameroun (Africa). In the U.S. in 1966, the percentage of deaths falling in the fifty-year-old-and-above age group was 81 percent; in the seventy-year-old-and-above, it was 49 percent. In the Cameroun in 1964–65, percentages for the corresponding age groups were 14 and 2 respectively.

Even granting a much higher infant mortality rate in the Cameroun, there is still a high death rate among adults who have important responsibilities to perform in the community. Almost everyone has died before the age of sixty. This means that death is a constantly disruptive factor; it comes frequently to those who are valuable producers in a society which is smaller and more intimate than ours. When a man dies in a tribal society, its very principle of existence is threatened.

In a massive industrial society such as Great Britain or the U.S., the event of death is postponed for the vast majority of its members until the highly active years of life are past. Death does not usually occur until the individual has discharged his responsibilities to both family and the larger society. As one gets older, one becomes progressively disengaged from responsibilities. So from the point of view of the society, there is a marked reduction in the degree of disruption to the social system owing to death. A person's death in the U.S. is now increasingly an affair which is peripheral to the concerns of the larger society; it is becoming a private event important only to a few individuals. The society is not threatened or deprived of a major contributor because too many live past the time when they are contributors.

It is evident, then, that what death is or means will vary drastically in various societies when there is a significant difference in the frequency of death to those who are actively engaged in social responsibilities, and when there are differences in the size of the societies. This is true without even considering the enormous differences in beliefs about the nature of reality in societies, which obviously affect their view of death and an individual's attitude toward it. Apparently the strain on the individual in Western industrial societies is increasing. His death does not matter socially, but he still has a unique concern and involvement with his own life. It is going to end, and he has to face this with less guidance and support from the society than he used to have. For belief in an afterlife is breaking down in Western societies, and there is no consensus to give confidence in the validity of any set of beliefs about death.

The question of the meaning of death is a legitimate one, however, over and above any social problems, personal breakdowns, or attempts to overcome social dislocations. Nor does this question have its basis only in the belief system of a society. Its fundamental ground is in the running together of two facts: we know that we will die, and we care about ourselves. How should we regard death?

SECTION II

What death means varies not only with the social setting but, as we have said, with the beliefs that are held about the nature of reality. This greatly affects our evaluation of the Christian belief in an afterlife, both morally and in terms of its credibility. Christianity by its portrait of God gives a people a view of death which it did not have before; God's reality helps specify what he overcomes by his gift of an afterlife. The gospel is not an answer to a problem specifiable utterly apart from any reference to God. The death which is overcome by life cannot be fully described without reference to the kind of life which God gives.

The Christian belief in an afterlife, therefore, does not make direct contact with the concerns about death which grow largely out of the social needs of a particular society. It is not especially addressed to these problems, though they are genuine ones: How do we keep a society going in which death is a terribly disruptive force? How do we cope with the needs of the dying in a society in which death is socially insignificant, yet personally a terrible reality? It is not, in other words, an answer to problems which get defined simply by a sociological study of societies or by an empirical study of the psychic needs of individuals in different social settings.[8]

When the meaning of death has not been influenced and penetrated by any consideration of the reality of a Christian God, the claim of a resurrected body and a life in the kingdom of God seems utterly stupid and cheap. When isolated, it is utterly unwarranted and cheap because it seems to reflect an inability to face death. God then becomes a *deus ex machina.*

Let us then consider what death means when viewed within the framework of the reality of a Christian God. To begin with, it is a good thing that human beings die, notwithstanding the fact that many die tragically and some die before they are old. It is a blessing that this life is limited in duration, not because it is not good and is to be denigrated, but because this kind of life cannot satisfy. Were it to go on as it now is on this earth, with what we are and with what is available, it would not satisfy our aspirations and potential. This life as it now is, were it to continue indefinitely, would become a dreary business. Consider, for example, how in India escape from this life, not its prolongation, is the problem. This life, when viewed as continuing indefinitely in successive reincarnations, is thought to be a bondage. Or consider the Faust legend, in which he is given the power by Satan to explore and experience the entire range of human life; in time, he grows weary and loses his zest. Or consider Kierkegaard's remarkable description of the "aesthete," the great boredom which is the disease of this kind of existence and which is staved off again and again by desperate means to avoid facing the fact that such a life is without validity. Sheer longevity then, is not an answer to death, because longevity is not an answer to life.

Many people in fact do not live long enough to become weary of this life; indeed, many who do live a long life do not attain the conviction that this life cannot satisfy our aspirations. But this may well be because our life is in fact of limited duration. Because there is only an allotted time, what we do have remains sweet, fascinating, and engaging. Nonetheless, it should be clear that Christianity does not offer an afterlife to meet the fear of *this* life's coming to an end. *This* life's ending is a blessing, a blessing which God confers on all people, whether they believe in him or not, whether they regard it as a blessing or not.[9]

Death is a blessing because it can also be an occasion for a more realistic assessment of oneself and such an assessment is a pathway to a recognition of the reality of God. As Barth points out, our allotted time has two boundaries: a beginning and an end. We are not particularly anxious about the fact that we once did not exist. When we look, however, toward the opposite direction, to the fact that one day we will not be, for many there is a touch of dread, of anxiety, or of uneasiness. This may be because we have during our lifetime accumulated guilts, regrets, and failures. By putting a time limit on an unjustified life, death has a "sting." One dreads to meet one's end when one's life is unjustified. So a time limit forces one to examine oneself and to consider what to do with an unjustified life. Clearly the fact of death does not impose a great burden on one who feels he can justify his life; the end poses no more problem for such a person than the fact that he begins. But the higher one's conception of one's obligations, and the less one condones fail-

ures, the more difficult it is to justify one's life.[10] Death's sting
is proportionate to one's yardstick. A major part of Christianity's
view of our life is that God justifies it and thereby removes the
sting of death. So the sting of death can lead one to look to God
for relief.

But apart from any anxiousness that results from an unjustified life, the very shortness of life itself calls for self-examination of one's life. Since life is of limited duration, it is rational
to ask (whether or not one does so), What should I do with what
I have? What is important? What is the truth of the reality about
us so that I can judge rightly what to do with my life? Death is
a blessing in that it calls us to examine the reality about us and
of ourselves in relation to it. Such an investigation (as we will
see) can lead one to find God and to enter into a path which
leads to the consummation of love.

Thirdly, death is a blessing because it threatens a *de facto*
position and a *de facto* worth. It logically means that one is but
one item among other realities, without unique ontological
status; it logically means that our experiential solipsism is a
distortion of reality. Death can thus be a spur to get one to ask,
What do I amount to? And the realistic answer is that one is but
one particular among many others, but that one is incapable of
sustaining an experience of oneself or others in that way. Death
then is a threat to a *de facto* self; but the Christian afterlife is
not a promise of perpetuation of a *de facto* self. Quite to the
contrary, the life which God seeks to confer on us is the consummation of the *moral* life. Such an afterlife does not remove the
dread and anxiousness that arise from the desire to continue
one's *de facto* existence.

The Christian afterlife, then, does not tell us not to worry
about death, nor that death is not real, nor if real not permanent. Christianity teaches us to accept death because this life
cannot satisfy and an allotted time helps makes this time precious. It teaches that death cannot keep us from attaining a
justified life and it drives us to seek one. It teaches us that an
allotted time means that we should investigate the reality

around us and ourselves in relation to it to determine how we are to use a limited time wisely. But an afterlife is not intended to rid us of that fear of death which arises from a *de facto* estimate of ourselves; it does not save one's *de facto* person from extinction. It promises the consummation of a moral perception and relation.

It should be clear that a person can be a good Christian and still be afraid of death, or at least in the process of dying become frightened. A *de facto* concern is not fully eradicated in this life, so that even a saintly person, much less a good Christian, can have his *de facto* concern swell up and take over his attention completely, and so fail to die well. But this is no greater or less a moral failing than other ways in which a good person, or a saint, may fail to be moral. Likewise one may die well without a Christian understanding of death, that is, without belief in a consummation of love. One may do this because one is moral and *at the time* not overcome with *de facto* self-concern. One may even die well, in the sense of not making a fuss and being resigned to it, from sheer weariness, or welcome death because of the severity of pain.

Our final point in this estimate of death from within the framework of the reality of God is that death is not a punishment. This is of course to depart from what is usually said by Christian theologians and preachers. Death is often referred to as the wages of sin. Whatever this extraordinarily involved Biblical phrase might mean, it should not mean that death is a punishment. By "punishment" I mean the inflicting of injury as an act of revenge, or suffering inflicted as a means of extracting payment or recompense in return for injury.

The view of love we have developed means that our destiny is an indwelling love. Punishment can get one closer to that goal. We ourselves, when outraged by another, might get rid of our resentment by inflicting injury or by allowing punishment to be inflicted, and thereby enhance the possibility of establishing a better relationship with another. But our Father does not harbor resentments at the way we treat each other or for our ungrateful neglect of him. He does not have any resentment to purge by inflicting injury, so that no such catharsis is necessary before God is able to seek a reconciliation.

Another way to advance toward the goal of indwelling love is for the outraged party not to punish but to sacrifice himself; that is, to suffer the outrage without resentment but with profound love. In the New Testament, Christ is said to have died for our sins; that is, God voluntarily suffers because of our sins and on our behalf. Were he to punish us, Christ would to that extent not be the Lamb of God who bears the sins of the world.[11]

Death is not a punishment, but a judgment of this life and our lives. As already pointed out, this life is of limited extent because it is unable to satisfy us and in it we are unable to attain the goal of a consummation of love. But death also heralds another truth. Our life is judged to be invalid because it is, and cannot fully escape from the unreality of, a *de facto* position and the outrage it thereby commits to other realities. It is a life of death, that is, a life of isolation from a true relation with others, and so it is to end. We have this time to give up our *de facto* stance; that is, willingly to desire that this life of isolation come to an end. If we do not, even it is taken away from us, and the loss is complete (". . . from him who has not, even what he has will be taken away"—Mark 4:25).

But though death is a judgment, Christ's death for the sins of the world (not just for believers' sins) means that we are loved by God. He does not hate us for what we are or have been (our particular sins) nor for our occupying a *de facto* position. This, and our weakness and vulnerability, our longing to be loved as particulars and to be attached, are perceived. It is a perception that causes him suffering. This we learn from Christ, from his voluntary suffering at the hands of men; as God incarnate, he forgave men on the cross, though he is treated outrageously.

God's suffering means that no injury which men receive, either from one another or from the natural world, no suffering that is endured as one strives for attainments and for love, is a punishment from God. Even though some suffering may be from the hand of God, it is not a punishment. That God does not punish is a benefit all men live under whether they believe in him or not. Yet even though suffering is not a punishment, many people do regard or at least have regarded suffering as a punishment.[12] Knowledge of Christ is therefore a great blessing. It removes this anxiety.

The removal of the sting of death, and the removal of all suffering, including death, as a punishment, does not mean that we will not suffer and die. That we all must do. Even Christ did not escape suffering and death. Though he died voluntarily, he was mortal; for his kind of life was like our own, a life under judgment. Even though Christ was perfect—that is, able to be free of *de facto* self-concern and able to love perfectly—the consummation of love requires love to be returned. The disciples did not love him perfectly and many people hated Jesus. This life is under judgment as inadequate; for all its glories, for all that it is good (judged to be good as a reality by God its creator), it is nonetheless not the life God intends us to have permanently, since it cannot be consummated. It is to end.

The life we are to have is one we only glimpse now and again as we struggle free (usually only to a degree and for a short time) from a *de facto* position to one that hints of a mutual indwelling. Our present life is one where we begin to learn what it is to be limited, to be isolated and yet to yearn to be bound to others. This life is to be seen as being transformed by another seeping in, a replacement that does not and cannot take place fully without a new heaven and a new earth and new minds and bodies. So Christianity does not promise life beyond death; *this* life is limited in extent and it will end permanently. Only what has entered this life from the heart of God—the life which he himself enjoys—which we see in Jesus and know now in self-forgetful perception and especially in a mutual reception of one another will continue and be consummated. But for the rest, what it will be is a completely blank tablet, since we and our universe must be transformed for the consummation of love.

Christianity does not solve the problem of regrasping this life by its reinstatement after death; but it offers a vision of what life is, and a taste of what true living is. That life, now only tasted, and in serious conflict with the present, is said to be incapable of destruction because it is the life of God and to live in it fully is a destiny given to us by God.[13]

In the Christian vision of reality, God's love is a perfect love; that is, he sees us with utter clarity. We can come to see ourselves indirectly by our effect on him. That perfect reflection of us in him is Jesus Christ on a cross. That is our effect on him. The self that is us, which God loves and perceives with perfect clarity, is one that kills, destroys, and denies other realities so that it may be unique.

The Christian conception of God is that God asks of a person that he be the object of a perfect love, the proper object. The proper object is one that is not filled with a sense of grandeur and unique importance. But Christianity asks not only for humility. Humility can be attained without Christianity by the recognition of the reality of one's own death and that of others. The proper object of a perfect love is also one whose awareness is filled with the one who loves. One continues to exist, not conscious of oneself, but conscious of the lover.

Christianity thus combines our nothingness (the destruction of our false exaltation and worth) with the grandeur of being one who is loved perfectly and forever by God. It asks a person to perform the incredible feat of being both humble and an object precious to God. Jesus was both a carpenter and the divine eternal Son. He was apparently able to combine both in one consciousness: to be full of the reality of others, though he himself was one with the prime reality. The Christian ideal, or to use Kierkegaard's phrase, the "Knight of Faith," is one who has lost his false worth and uniqueness and is aware of himself only indirectly, because he is conscious only of the object of his devotion: God who loves perfectly.[14] One must lose one's life to find it.

Conclusion

It should be clear that life after death in Christianity under the interpretation I have given is not a doctrine to be entertained because of a self-centered fear of the loss of this life. Only a moral person can receive eternal life; and eternal life is not an arbitrary award, but is the consummation of the moral life. Clearly there is not any apparent ulterior motivation in one's desiring such consummation; for the reality one faces is one which is humiliating. God is the unique reality; we are realities only by his creation of us from nothing. The entranceway into his presence is by death of the unreality of our present perception; the reward is the good itself; that is, the perception of the reality that he is and the reality he has conferred on others. It is neither death that one seeks to escape, nor traditional hellfire, but the unreality of one's present position for that which is true. That this involves a consummation is indeed a reason for great joy; but this joy is not incompatible with being moral. It is a joy which comes only to those who seek to be moral (". . . to him who has will more be given . . ."—Mark 4:25).

Death, then, is not the interruption of the progress we have made toward the goal of a genuine recognition of the reality of others. Death is the complete destruction of the *de facto* life which we now have and which has been only partly overcome by the movement we have made from viewing all things from our point of view. What we seek is the end of a *de facto* life; what we want to come into fullness is the perfect awareness of the presence of God and that of others which has already begun. The more fully, clearly, and deeply we have perceived the presence of God, the greater is our confidence in the completion of the life which is now being received from a presence that is not of this world. The more we know his presence, the more we are assured that the kingdom will come. This hope and its ground we will now consider more fully.

Chapter Six

FAITH IN THE RESURRECTION:
How We Can Believe

*

The Christian basis for belief in the consummation of life in the kingdom of God has always been Jesus' resurrection. It is because he was raised by God that we can believe that we too will be raised to life in the kingdom that is to come. In spite of the stark reality of death, and the painful loss of loved ones, we can retain our hope in the resurrection of the dead and patiently endure their loss, because of Christ's resurrection. But on what basis or on what grounds can we believe in the resurrection of Christ? We have the New Testament reports of his appearances to his disciples; and we have a living chain of witnesses who have passed down to us the disciples' claim to having seen the risen Lord. Is this enough to establish his resurrection?

This is a very involved question, so we will proceed by separating its various strands. The resurrection of Christ is a miracle or "wonder," as the New Testament would put it. There have been extreme claims made, mostly in the early eighteenth century by the French *philosophes* (or social critics) such as Voltaire, and by nineteenth-century materialists, that miracles are impossible: the resurrection of Jesus could not have occurred because such events are contrary to the known laws of nature.

Today the objection to all miracles on the basis of the natural sciences cannot be sustained. The older view of known and unbreakable laws has been superseded. At present we do not pretend to know the final laws of the universe. The Newtonian world of known and fixed laws applicable universally without exception has been upset by quantum physics and relativity theory. We realize more than at any time since the early eighteenth century how much nature operates in a common-sense defying way. So we cannot rule out unusual phenomena, such as we find reported in the New Testament, simply by claiming that they are contrary to science and hence impossible.

A more formidable position than this was first formulated by David Hume in the late eighteenth century, and since then much further developed. He said in effect that we cannot claim that miracles are impossible. But we should not believe reports about their occurrence in ancient times; for in order to write history, we must judge what most likely happened in the past by what happens nowadays, and miracles do not now happen. Fraud, gullibility, sincere mistakes, and the like are always more plausible as hypotheses to explain ancient reports than that such reported miracles occurred.

This principle is very powerful, because we do want to determine what happened in the past, not merely in religion, but in all aspects of the past of the human race. Much of the material from the past which we use to reconstruct historical events and write history is saturated with tall tales, fables, and legends. A critical historian must use his own present-day experience in order to evaluate the materials from the past to judge what most likely occurred. Since fraud, ignorance, superstition and gullibility are so common, and since few if any historians claim to have experienced any miracles today, it is very difficult to be consistent in rejecting miracles in some places while retaining them in the critical appraisal of the New Testament. If one does affirm the miraculous in the New Testament accounts, it is by an act of faith rather than on the basis of critical history.

Much of today's skepticism concerning the resurrection of Christ is the result of the assumption that the only way it can be affirmed is by critical history. I do not agree with this assumption. But how then can we today believe it by faith? I will argue that we may affirm it today because of our ability to perceive the presence of God. By moving away from our selfish perspective and thereby becoming aware of the reality of other things, and by forsaking the world, we can upon hearing the gospel find ourselves being nourished by contact with an invisible presence. That perception of his presence is our sheet anchor. It does not solve historical problems, but it does enable us to have a powerful faith in the resurrection of Christ, and hence confidence in the consummation of love in the kingdom of God. Let us now consider this in detail.

SECTION I

In the New Testament there are several accounts of the appearance of the risen Lord to his disciples. They raise many critical problems for an historian. For example, it has proved exceedingly difficult, if not impossible, to make them harmonize with one another. There are discrepancies as to times, sequences, and places so that the accounts do not bear the mark of straightforward reports given by eyewitnesses and passed on and preserved with great care by their hearers. Also, an incident such as Jesus' appearance to two followers on the road to Emmaus, where Jesus is not recognized by them until he breaks the bread at mealtime, is quite convincingly interpreted as a communion meditation in which the living Lord is said to be present to the believer in the breaking of bread, and not an actual report of an appearance on the road to Emmaus.

This is just a sample of the critical problems connected with the appearance stories in the Gospels. We need not pursue them any further because I want to avoid the following sort of argument.

FIRST SPEAKER: We believe in the resurrection because the disciples saw him and told us about it.
SECOND SPEAKER: But how do you know they saw him?
FIRST SPEAKER: The Bible says they saw him.

SECOND SPEAKER: But that is doubtful because the accounts of
                   his appearances recorded in the Bible do
                   not harmonize with each other; some
                   clearly are later additions (such as the Em-
                   maus incident).
FIRST SPEAKER: But you simply cannot account for the dis-
                   ciples' behavior after Jesus' death unless
                   they did see him alive again.

There is a reply to this argument, and likewise a rejoinder to the
reply, and so on indefinitely. We thus find ourselves bogged
down in an interminable historical investigation to work out the
most likely historical reconstruction for what did happen back
in Palestine.

This discussion is not only interminable, but we wonder how
a firm, strong, robust affirmation of the resurrection of Jesus can
ever emerge from the probabilities and counter-probabilities of
historical reconstruction. We all know that historical events are
essential to Christianity, but how are we to have a firm faith
when a crucial event such as the resurrection of Jesus seems to
lack historical evidence of such a quality as to enable us to give
wholehearted commitment to the gospel?

It seems to me that such a faith is possible if we can show that
the appearance stories are inessential and find another basis for
belief in the resurrection. We can maintain belief in Jesus'
resurrection without affirming or denying the historical accuracy of the appearance stories as they are found in the New
Testament.

Section II

The position that is now to be presented relies on the particular (though thoroughly traditional) view of the content of the
gospel which has been presented so far in this book. God is love,
and a particular kind of love, consisting as he does of three
centers of power, each of which so completely puts its entire
power (or person) at the disposal of the others that they possess
one another (or indwell in one another). This giving is so com-

plete that they are one God: Father, Son, and Holy Spirit. This love of Father, Son, and Spirit is also directed to the creation, especially to men who are forgiven sinners, and who are promised that the love they now receive from him and which they themselves at present are able to return and share with one another only feebly will be perfected in a never-ending love after death.

As far as the resurrection of Christ is concerned, it seems clear that the only matter which is crucial for the maintenance of the gospel, as I have just formulated it, is that Jesus, who once lived and died in Palestine, is now alive. Were he not now alive, then our conception of God's love would not be of a trinitarian love which became incarnate and which seeks to have us partake in the life of the Trinity itself. Were Jesus not alive, there would be no Trinity and the view of love it portrays would be incapable of statement. Were there no such love in which we might participate, then there would be no possibility that the love between ourselves which is so imperfect and feeble could be consummated in a perfect and eternal way.

It is not so clear, however, that the resurrected Jesus had to *appear*. What if the following occurred? The corpse returned to life, suitably transformed, and went to the Father without anyone's seeing him on earth. There would still be a resurrection (Jesus is now alive) without any appearances. Now one might object to this possibility that the resurrection appearances are necessary because without them the disciples would not have become convinced of the truth of the gospel.

This seems a very plausible statement. There was a remarkable change in the disciples' behavior. Very broadly expressed, in the Gospels of the New Testament they often misunderstood Jesus, and they often wavered in their loyalty to him. Later we find them far more insightful about the gospel and firm in their convictions. So on this sort of basis, it might be claimed that they must have seen him.

But we must draw still another distinction. We must distinguish between the situations of the disciples and ourselves. We living today might believe that Jesus is now alive (that he was resurrected from the dead and continues to live), and not believe this because we rely on the soundness of the stories we have in the Bible reporting his resurrection *appearances*. We might say that whether the stories are to be judged to be probable or improbable is a matter for historical study. A negative outcome there does not falsify the claim that Jesus was resurrected (and is now alive). That is, Jesus could have risen from the dead and have not been seen, or have not been seen as has been reported in the Gospel narratives.

This could be said because the ground on which one believes in Jesus' resurrection is not the reports about his postcrucifixion *appearances*. One might believe in the gospel (a crucified and risen Jesus, now living) for reasons other than the reports of appearances. For example, it is a gospel of a divine love that becomes incarnate for our sakes, suffers for our sakes, and promises us that we will be united eternally with him. God so loves us as to want that love to be fully received (which is the same as for us to be in a condition of fully returning it) and to be fully shared between us. That gospel requires a resurrected Jesus and resurrected believers; without them there is no consummation of love. One can believe in this gospel primarily because one finds oneself responding with love to such a love. That is, because one has forsaken the world, and has an emptiness which craves to be filled, one finds that a presence is mediated to one by this gospel. One experiences that emptiness touched and partly filled by an invisible reality. This reality is brought to one by the gospel that proclaims a living risen Lord, who is able to establish this contact only because he is indeed the living risen Lord. One's ground for belief, for assurance that Christ has risen, is the loving presence now mediated by the gospel account. And that gospel account can be stated without commitment to the accuracy of the resurrection *appearance stories*. It cannot be stated without the resurrection. Because that gospel fills a void, it awakens faith in the resurrection.

Thus one can believe in the resurrection of Jesus, have a

sound and compelling basis for a dynamic and wholehearted faith, without founding that faith on the historical accuracy of the appearances as recorded in the New Testament. When the appearance narratives are considered solely in terms of their value as evidence for the truth of the gospel, they are not essential. Today one can believe in the resurrection without being committed to the postresurrection appearance accounts, because they are not needed as evidence, and they do not add anything to the content of the gospel.

This position may seem oversubtle. So perhaps it is well to ask the reader to recall how he came to have faith. In many instances it was probably through an exposure to the content of the gospel: the story of God's love in Jesus, who was sent to us by the Father to die for our sins, and whom the Father vindicated by raising him from the dead. But this account was not regarded merely as some statements to be affirmed, but awakened a living faith; that is, established *contact* with the Spirit or presence of God who so acted. The character of the one known by faith is given by the gospel story; and faith is contact with the reality so described. Although that gospel story says that Jesus appeared to the disciples, and we have some recorded narratives of the appearances, we do not have to hold to those recorded narratives. Our reason for belief in the resurrection is more direct, immediate, and personal: it is our own experience of the living Lord in our contact with a presence mediated to us by the gospel of a God who sent Jesus and who raised him from the dead.

A believer is often sidetracked from reliance on a living faith. It can happen this way. Someone asks him, "Why do you believe in God?" He may reply, "Because of Jesus who loved us and died for us, and was raised from the dead." The one asks, "But why believe in his resurrection?" It is at this point that the other may get sidetracked by giving the convenient reply, "His disciples saw him." This opens the way to the interminable historical discussion that gets lost in probabilities and counterprobabilities, and from which faith—a rich sense of the presence of God—does not arise. A living faith is what we started with, and from which we must not depart in search for some other foundation for our convictions. It is because of our contact with God—a response of love to a portrayal of his love—that we believe. As long as one does not leave that base, one may take part in historical discussions and reconstructions with much profit, but not with the expectation that one's primary commitment depends on documentation of the narratives of Jesus' appearances.

All of this has been stated on the assumption that the appearance stories are being considered simply and solely as *evidence* for the gospel, as a ground for having faith, and considered specifically from the standpoint of their role as evidence for us who live today.

We must now consider the situation of the disciples. Here too we will examine the appearance stories strictly in terms of their role of providing evidence, but in this case, providing evidence for the disciples. We assume in this case that they were able to understand and receive the content of the gospel before Jesus allegedly appeared to them. In other words, they did not need actually to see the risen Lord in order to know *what* the gospel was.[1]

Now the appearances, did they take place, would be evidence or good grounds for them to believe in the truth of the gospel. But did the disciples need such grounds? We might try to answer this question by asking ourselves, Is it possible to account for their belief that Jesus had risen from the dead and is now alive, unless we grant that he appeared to them? It is utterly clear on historical grounds that the disciples believed in the resurrection. But it seems much less clear that the only or the best way to account for their belief is that he appeared to them. It might be possible to account for their conviction that he is alive on the same type of grounds as one today has, viz., the content of the gospel and a perception in it of a perfect love and a promise of its consummation to which one responds with believing love. It might be necessary in the disciples' case to add to this an empty tomb with no appearances, or visions of Jesus similar to Paul's vision on the road to Damascus, or a combination of an empty tomb and visions. There are lots of possibilities for a historical construction to account for their belief in the resurrection without any appearances. So if the resurrection appearances are considered only as *evidence* for the resurrection, then they are not crucial.

On the other hand, historical study might show that appearances (that is, that the disciples believed they saw him) were necessary to account for the disciples' conviction that Jesus rose. That might be the best historical reconstruction. Nonetheless that still might not be *our* ground today for *our* belief in the resurrection. We could say: "It looks as though the best way to account for the disciples' belief in the resurrection is that they believed that they saw him. But that isn't the foundation of my own belief in the resurrection. My faith is based upon the effect on me of the content of the gospel; it creates in me the conviction that I am in contact with God's presence." So in either case the appearance stories need not be *our* basis for belief in the resurrection. Historical reconstruction on this point can go either way without our faith in the resurrection being undermined.

We can, then, leave the issue of what the disciples' grounds were for belief that Jesus is alive open to historical study. We do not need to know why they believed to know what they believed: their testimony to a resurrection—that Jesus is now alive—is utterly clear. And we can respond to that view of love —a God who perceives us with compassion, and in whose life, death, and resurrection we perceive a love that calls for and promises a consummation of love—without knowing *why* they believed that he was alive.

Section III

Let me now bring the argument together and make some general remarks about the relation of faith to critical history.

If we assume the worst, namely, that we cannot by historical investigation and reconstruction determine what the disciples needed in order to believe the gospel, we are not in the position of having our faith today dangling without sufficient foundation. Nor are we in the position of having to choose *on historical grounds* one historical reconstruction instead of another (all of which are speculative because of the scarcity and quality of the data); for we today have the content of the gospel (however it was originally gained) and we have reason to believe it independently of the disciples' reasons (which are unknown to us).

This position affirms that the gospel has its origin in history; it came from there somehow. But we do not have to recover by historical study its historical basis and reproduce all the steps in its formulation, *however useful that might be*. We do not need to be troubled about the validity of the gospel because of the scarcity of historical data. Instead of starting by trying to isolate some historical data and from that data trying to work toward the gospel, we have begun with the gospel and asked, Precisely what events as a minimum must have occurred in order for us to continue to affirm the gospel which has been passed down to us by a believing community? Clearly the gospel entails that there was a Jesus, that he was not immoral, that he died on a cross; but as we have argued, it is not necessary that he appeared to anyone on earth. What has to be affirmed as having occurred is affirmed. Historical investigation could undermine the gospel and hence force us to abandon our affirmation, should it determine that an event which must be true if the gospel is true, in fact did not occur. It may also indicate that some events did occur, and thus show that some of the necessary conditions for the truth of Christianity in fact did occur (such as Jesus' death on a cross). Historical study, however, need not certify all the events or perhaps any of them, in order for one to believe the gospel and to affirm the events which it entails. They must have occurred for the gospel to be true, but the assertion of their occurrence does not have to be certified by historical evidence.

These observations are crucial for us today. A high-theology seems to be incapable of being propounded by those engaged in historical investigation on the basis of historical study in spite of some prodigious attempts and programs—at least this is one of the factors which seem to be involved in the current talk about a crisis in Biblical theology. Therefore I am proposing that we take a traditional view of the gospel and indeed affirm that which we must affirm about events, and deeds, and the character of Jesus, but that we do so without thinking we must have all this certified by historical study before we have a right to affirm it. We have grown used to the idea that the gospel is not a philosophy, nor a statement to be vindicated and based on philosophical speculation. We need to grow used to the idea that it is not to be conferred on us nor certified for us by critical historical reconstructions either.

What is necessary for faith in the resurrected Lord is discipline. If our selfish perspective has been penetrated by the reality of others, and if we have forsaken the world—both of which are extremely difficult tasks—then we can upon hearing the gospel find ourselves being nourished by contact with an invisible presence. The gospel which mediates to us his presence is a gospel about an incarnate Son who died and is now alive. We can believe the claim that he is alive because the emptiness which craves to be filled is touched and partly filled by an invisible reality brought to one by the gospel which proclaims a living risen Lord. Because we know his living presence through its being portrayed to us and received by us in the gospel, we can believe the gospel of a living risen Lord whose kingdom shall come.[2]

Chapter Seven

WHAT WE ARE TO
EXPECT FROM GOD

*

We have argued that the presence of God can be perceived indirectly by a person who is moving from his *de facto* stance and who has forsaken the world. It is contact with his presence which enables us to face the reality of death and which undergirds our faith in the resurrection of Christ. It gives us confidence in the hope of a glorious fulfillment of the creation beyond this present heaven and earth. The more our life is disciplined by attentiveness to others, and the more we cultivate an awareness of the inability of the world to give us a fulfillment which we crave, the deeper and clearer is our awareness of his presence.

But does such a disciplined religious life protect us from harm in this life? For our faith is frequently sorely tried by the illness of our loved ones or of ourselves, by tragic accidents, by many disappointments with our family life and with our work. Things do go wrong. We need, then, to consider what God does for us in this life, and what we are to expect from him.

This question has a special relevance today because of the use to which the supernatural is put, especially in America. For many, religion is a way to get God's help. There are literally thousands of people who will testify to miraculous aid. A businessman will tell you of how he received guidance in what to bid on a contract; an actress will tell you how prayer helped her cry for a movie scene when she had failed to cry several times and her career was in jeopardy; a car salesman will tell you that his success in selling cars comes from his faith in God. Hundreds of groups appeal to people with promises of divine assistance in attaining health, and supply you with testimonials of successful cures. Freud's theory that God functions as a crutch for people who cannot stand on their own feet does not begin to convey the brashness of the phenomena. Plugging into the supernatural is more like the greedy exploitation of a bonanza. And the impression is conveyed that the more things you believe God can do for you in this life, the more religious you are. A really religious person looks to God for daily care in every venture, and thinks God gives success and protection from all harm to those who believe the most and pray the hardest.

The problem is compounded today by an occult explosion. There is a resurgence of magic, astrology, witchcraft, spiritualism (messages from the dead), mysticism in a myriad of forms —with Eastern cult gurus too numerous to keep track of, and even a dash of Satanism.

We noted in dealing with the resurrection that at one time science was used as a way to declare that all miracles were impossible. With changes in science, it cannot be used to pull the rug out from under all unusual phenomena. But in the same way, it cannot be used to rule out all occult phenomena in one fell swoop either. So the problem for us is that once you let the "supernatural" in at all, how do you draw the line between what is permissible and what is not? If you accept, for example, miracles, demons, angels, and telepathy, then why not astrology, fortune-telling, out-of-body experience, premonitions of the future, spiritualism, ghosts, witches, werewolves, and vampires? And if the miraculous is possible, then with all sorts of accounts of healing in Scripture, why not look to the divine as a source of health, protection, and success? How can you find a way to distinguish good religion from bad religion, that is, between what we rightly ought to ask God to do for us, and what is really an attempt to exploit him? But to handle our original question of what God does for us in this life, we will first have to deal more generally with the subject of Jesus' miracles.

SECTION I

In the New Testament we find it recorded that Jesus performed mighty "wonders and signs." He healed the blind and made the lame to walk. He walked on water, and changed water into wine. He raised Lazarus from the dead, and was himself raised from the dead. A rationalist such as David Friedrich Strauss in the Introduction to his *Life of Jesus* roundly declared:

> We may summarily reject all miracles, prophecies, narratives of angels and demons, and the like, as simply impossible and irreconcilable with the known and universal laws which govern the course of events.[1]

It is exceedingly difficult to imagine a reconstruction of the life of Jesus which presents his ministry devoid of all miracles, and which at the same time gives us a Lord who is to be worshiped. And neither by present-day science nor by any other means can we rule out the possibility of miracles.

On the other hand, if miracles are possible, then Jesus is not unique. The history of the religions of mankind is full of miracles, including walking on water and resurrection of the dead. Jesus' power to work wonders might give Jesus some authority but not unique authority. We have to find something between the extremes of no miracles at all and having so many miracles that they dissipate the uniqueness of Christ.

We avoid both extremes if we examine the way Jesus' powers were regarded in the New Testament itself. To begin with, there was no claim that miraculous powers were unique to Jesus; he was not the only person thought to have been able to heal and to cast out demons. Secondly, the ability to perform miracles did not mean a person was from God. We nowadays usually think as did John Locke who said that "he who comes with a message from God to be delivered to the world, cannot be refused belief if he vouches his mission by a miracle . . ."[2] But this was not so in New Testament times. For people then, miraculous power meant that a person was either from God or from Satan; either one could confer unusual powers on a person. We even have a warning in Mark 13:22 against diabolical wonder-working: "False Christs and false prophets will arise and show signs and wonders, to lead astray, if possible, the elect."

The way to tell whether a person performing wonders was from God or Satan was whether he was a good person or not. To us today, it seems obvious that Jesus was a good person. In Jesus' day it was clear to many of the religious leaders that Jesus was not a good person; for he repeatedly broke the Jewish Law. The Gospel narratives are replete with instances of his controversies with the Pharisees and the Scribes over his actions in relation to the Law. He claimed, for example, to be Lord of the Sabbath, that is, to have authority over the Law, which they considered to be a clear demonstration of his evil. Perhaps his strongest claim in this regard was the claim that "before Abraham was, I am"; that is, he claimed to take precedence over the first lawgiver.

But his disciples recognized or accepted his authority. Since he broke the Law, the acceptance of him as an authority from God could not be established by his miracles. How then did they come to accept his authority? Apparently the disciples judged Jesus to be a good person from his compassion for those in need, from the purity of his life, from his teaching, despite the fact that he sometimes broke the Law. But all this does not make him divine or unique. It only shows that he was not from the devil, but was a saintly person, and a revealer, as were the prophets of old, of God's will.

So miracles could not establish his authority as one from God. But his miracles are nonetheless important. They establish *how far* his authority extends. Thus, if one judges him to be a good person, then miracles show the *extent* of his authority or of his power. They reveal to those who recognize his goodness what he has authority over. This interpretation is suggested by the disciples' remark, when Jesus saved their ship from sinking in a storm, that "even wind and sea obey him" (Mark 4:41). They knew that many other things obeyed him; now they learned that *even* the wind and sea are under his authority. They had already learned that he had power over demons (or illness). They had learned that he had power over sin; for he had used his power to heal to exhibit that his authority also extended over sin (when he forgave a paralytic and was challenged over his authority to forgive sins; see Mark 2:1–12). Now they learned that his power or authority extended over the wind and the sea. Eventually they came to learn that he had power or authority even over death. The progressive unveiling of the extent of his authority culminates in their confession of him as Lord, a title hitherto reserved for God. And if we interpret the cryptic remarks concerning the destruction and rebuilding of the temple in three days in John 2 as a claim of authority over the sacrifices for sin that occurred there, we see that his miracles can be construed as *part* of a revelation or unveiling of the extent of his authority. That is, they are not isolated phenomena in his ministry, but one manner in which the extent of his authority or power is revealed. It is an unveiling which is to be completed with his return when all things shall be seen to be put "under his feet." So I suggest that the miraculous in the New Testament accounts of Jesus is not to be used to establish that he was from God—as did John Locke, following a long tradition—but one fashion in which he exhibited the extent of his authority or power.

SECTION II

Now I suggest we follow this New Testament order: to move not from miracles to belief in Jesus, but from Jesus, whose goodness we apprehend, to the apprehension of the extent of his power. The issue for us then becomes, How far does it extend? Does it extend over illness, over wind and sea, over sin and death? How can we answer these questions?

It seems that we cannot call upon a view of science, as did

David Strauss, to claim that all unusual phenomena are impossible. They may be unlikely, but not impossible. On the other hand, the possibility that people might have the power to perform unusual phenomena is too general to be of any use to us. It does not help us to determine from the New Testament records just how great his powers actually were. The possibility of miraculous or unusual powers does not help a Biblical scholar determine in detailed critical study of the Bible just what did happen in a particular reported incident. For example, the episode of stilling the wind and the sea may have been written after the disciples had become convinced of the resurrection, and then read back into his earthly ministry, as their confession and testimony to the extent of his power. It would be a way to affirm by faith that Jesus' power extends over all of nature, and that this will become evident with the Parousia or second coming, when Christ's rule over all things will become manifest in the kingdom of God. So if you want to determine precisely how far Jesus' power did extend in his earthly ministry, belief in the possibility of miracles or extraordinary powers *as such* will not tell you.

Let us then try another tack. When a rationalist wants to purge the miraculous out of the New Testament, what is his motivation? In Bultmann's case (in contrast to David Strauss) he wants to make the genuine gospel apparent and available for belief today. He wants to rid it of its husk of bad religion and bad science, of belief in supernatural assistance and protection, as well as of a worn-out theory of a three-storey universe with angels and demons. Now if that is what one is after, a way to distinguish the gospel from bad religion, then I think there is a better principle available by which to draw the line than the rationalist's principle of denying the miraculous. It is based on an anecdote related by Simone Weil.

> . . . [A]n ascetic, after fourteen years spent in solitude, returned to see his family. His brother asked him what he had acquired in that time. So he led his brother down to a river and crossed it on foot before his very eyes. The brother hailed a ferryman,

crossed by boat, handed over a penny, and said to the ascetic, "Is it worth while spending fourteen years' effort in order to acquire what I can obtain by the payment of a penny?"[3]

From this I suggest that we are to look to God for that which only he can give. If it is available elsewhere, we are not to ask for it, even though he can provide it. One thing which only he can give us is genuine goodness or holiness; for only he is holy. The other thing which only he can give us is his kingdom. If we are busy asking him for other things, then we can miss the primary things. Doing well in business, finding health, seeking an expanded consciousness, begging protection from all danger are not related to seeking holiness or the kingdom.

The Lord's Prayer is our model for what we are to expect of God and to ask for in this life. We are to ask that the kingdom come, his will to be done here as in heaven. We are to ask for forgiveness—and for daily bread. (Notice that it is only for *daily* bread, not for a surplus, that we are to ask). And though we get daily bread by our own labor, it is not an exception to the principle we are using. We can expect and ask that the world be so arranged that as we seek goodness and the kingdom we do not necessarily have to court starvation but will have the opportunity by our labor to receive our daily bread. Let us then read, Allow us to seek our daily bread. We are to ask not to be led into temptation, that is, not to be exposed to an evil which can destroy our devotion to him, as we find in the temptations Jesus faced in the wilderness, in the garden of Gethsemane, and on the cross. This is the temptation whereby the joy of God's presence is utterly absent, and one experiences the affliction of being forsaken. But there is no petition to escape suffering as such. Instead he taught us that rain falls on the just and the unjust alike; that is, the universe created by God, which is still under his providential care, is indifferent to the moral qualities of people. You can be a good person and find things go badly for you; an evil one, and find things work out well, and vice versa.

The petitions about daily bread and temptation are closely

related. In Robert Coles' reports on religion among the rural poor,[4] we find the poor fervently praying for strength to endure the struggles of daily life. They need the inspiration of his Spirit just to keep physically going and not to give up. They need him to lift and strengthen their very bodies. They have been driven by severe poverty and cruel conditions, by the terrible torment of seeing their children and spouses humiliated, to totter on the brink of cursing life, which is the same as to curse God. Like Job they are tempted to "curse God, and die." To pray for bodily strength to continue the struggle to earn their daily bread is also to pray to overcome the temptation to curse God and die.

These chaste limits in our petitions are to be observed, even though there is the ascription of abundant power to God (". . . thine is the kingdom, and the power, and the glory"). So the principle suggested is not based on limitations in Jesus' power or God's power, but on limits we are to impose on ourselves in what we are to ask for, so that we not lose the narrow way that leads to purity and the kingdom. The stress on those things which we indeed want, and which can sometimes be gained by other means—such as wealth, prestige, health—is a stress on what are not religious goals. Even if religion—Christian or otherwise—is employed by people and testified to by them as a way that works to gain these things, they are nonetheless engaged in bad religion. Mark 13:22 (the "false prophets" verse mentioned before) is a good warning against the employment of Christianity, other religions, or bizarre techniques for any goal but that of genuine goodness.

The practices of praying for the sick and for guidance in our daily lives are not ruled out by any means. What is ruled out is the picture of God as an emperor who dispenses personal favors to those who pray to him or use some method to gain his attention. What we can expect from him with complete confidence, without exception, is the presence of his goodness to those who desire earnestly and with singleness of mind to be rid of their evil. If we turn our attention fully to him, that is, point ourselves in that direction by a forsaking of the world, then we find ourselves receiving a pure presence which absorbs our evil. And when we are ill, in severe pain, we can indeed rightly cry out to him for relief. And he may relieve us. But we also may not be relieved. For it is his primary concern that we enter the kingdom and that we learn to trust him and always expect good from him, but not expect special physical care or protection that never fails, and success in those things which are not within his exclusive domain.

On this basis we do not need to know the extent of Jesus' power or authority during his historic career. We approximate the condition of the disciples during his earthly ministry. They had to discern his goodness, through the veil of the Law he broke, if any miracle he performed were to count as establishing the extent of his authority. Without that discernment, miracles were of no use. So too we must discern his goodness, and desire ourselves to be perfect. Otherwise, alleged help in being healed, or alleged power to heal others, and speaking in tongues, help in being a financial success, and all the rest, however well attested to, are millstones around our neck. They do not advance a person one step toward the discernment of goodness or the earnest passionate desire for it.

If we earnestly long for God, that is, for that which alone can satisfy us, we find that this void is being filled. This is partly accomplished by the very discernment and contemplation of Jesus' goodness, the beauty of what he taught, and the beauty of the notion that he is indeed God's love for us. But we did not witness the resurrection; we only have reports that it happened —reports to the effect that this resurrection is a first fruit, a preview of the future of man and a new heaven and earth to come. So we have to trust that Jesus' power extends that far on the basis of the nourishment we now receive from God, largely through testimony about Jesus, as we hunger and thirst for righteousness. Just as the disciples had to follow him during his earthly career and to see his power unfold step by step, so too we have to wait to see that power made manifest when the final unveiling takes place. Meanwhile the testimony to the resurrection and the Parousia, and the nourishment we now receive, give us hope that his power and authority indeed extend so far as to make all things new.

This arrangement does not result from God's lack of compassion. On the contrary, it exists precisely because he is love. He desires us to have within ourselves a pure and unselfish relation to him and to all other realities; he desires us to be as he is. That presence cannot be known, that love cannot be within us and motivate us, except by being desired for its own sake. To desire God for any reason but his love is not to desire God. Though nothing is closer to us than God—for spirits may indwell in one another—nothing is farther away from us, unless we desire him. And because of this, the love of God is a suffering love: setting us at a distance by creating us as independent centers of reality, enduring every pain and evil which we suffer and cause, so that we may by our own wish and desire take our focus off ourselves, and desire his presence.

NOTES

*

CHAPTER ONE

1. The churches' neglect of men's condition is indeed a serious charge. It is true that men do not live by bread alone, just as it is true that they do not live without it either. But there is no easy resolution of this problem; for the problem is not merely to wed this world and the next, but *what* of this world is related to the next.

2. See the review of the Buber volume in "Library of Living Philosophers," *The Philosophical Review* (April, 1969), p. 276.

CHAPTER TWO

1. (New York: The Viking Press, 1963), pp. 188–189.

2. *Waiting on God*, trans. Emma Craufurd (London: Routledge and Kegan Paul Ltd., 1951), p. 1.

3. I expect that the novelist considers the capacity to perform this moral act of concentration in the face of imminent death to be partly the result of previous innumerable small acts. A person has the capacity for major moral acts because of previous, minor, unheroic, undramatic acts and the cultivation thereby of feelings and character. See Iris Murdoch, *The Sovereignty of Good* (New York: Schocken Books, Inc., 1971), pp. 36–37.

4. *The Prisoner and the Bomb* (New York: William Morrow and Company, Inc., 1971), pp. 12–13.

5. G. M. Wyburn, R. W. Pickford, and R. J. Hirst, *Human Senses and Perception* (Toronto, Canada: University of Toronto Press), 1964.

6. I am aware that there are many philosophical difficulties here,

especially in relation to the Mind-Brain Identity Theory. My own reasons for thinking the Mind-Brain Identity Theory is false may be found in my discussion note, "Tactile and Non-tactile Awarenesses," in *Mind* (October, 1969), pp. 567–70.

7. It could also be called moral solipsism, and it is capable of being interpreted as the essence of sin or of original sin.

8. They only need to be somewhat like ourselves to prevent uniqueness, for even under that minimal condition one can no longer view all things as orbiting around oneself only, which breaks the fantasy of experiential solipsism.

9. Sartre's character Roquentin in *Nausea* perceives the independence of things but it fills him with a sickly horror. But this is because he is not enough of a person for them to be in orbit around him or for him to release them; he lacks a sense of identity and sameness through time, so everything is fluid and unrelated.

A detailed comparison of Roquentin's experience and that of Cooper's is made in my article "Two Experiences of Existence," *International Philosophical Quarterly*, 1974.

10. In fact, to say how much worth, one needs something else to compare it with, and there is nothing else, since in the vision, all are valuable, without distinction, for it is their very independence, the acceptance of them as they are, which captivates one. Later, with a more complete description of love, some estimate of worth can be made.

11. They must attain perfect love, or approach it, for my true worth to be recognized.

12. There are several allusions by the narrator to the Trinity, the great Three-in-One.

13. It is of interest that on the cover of the paper edition she is portrayed with her eyes closed, and smiling; she does not perceive people as they are, including herself. On the back cover, her image is rent, suggesting destruction.

14. "Love as Perception of Meaning" in *Religion and Understanding*, ed. D. Z. Phillips (New York: The Macmillan Company, 1967), p. 151.

15. I have here introduced my own use of the common English word "particular" and its cognate "particularity." Since they will occur in important contexts throughout the rest of the book, let me call special attention to what I mean by them. I use the terms to mean the recognition of the reality of things independently of the distortion caused by our perception of them from our own point of view. To perceive things independently of our tastes, desires, preferences, and of their utility—in short, to release them from our orbit—is to perceive

them as particulars. In other words, to see ourselves as but one reality among many others is to recognize them as particulars; it is to recognize their particularity.

The justification of this usage is that one way in which we can control others, or put them into orbit around ourselves, is by classifying them according to type: see a thing as a chair, or a person as a neurotic. Their particular reality can thus be lost in the *general* type, and we then do not notice that though they can be so viewed and reduced, they can break these bounds and can be seen as themselves. The contrast between the particular and the general, which was first made important by Plato, is commented on near the end of this chapter where I criticize Plato's elevation of the general over the particular.

16. *Waiting on God*, p. 5.

17. "Love as Perception of Meaning" in *Religion and Understanding*, ed. Phillips, pp. 149–50.

18. Both to respect others' particularity and to help them, i.e., to prevent their suffering, introduces a possible conflict, should "help" mean changing them. This conflict, which Kierkegaard in the *Philosophical Fragments* calls an unhappy love, may not arise often in our experience, since we do not often perceive others' particularity. But it is another factor which complicates the move from a *de facto* position to a moral one, as we can violate the independence of others even when we seek to help them. It can be an intolerable helping.

19. New York: The Viking Press, 1966.

20. The true hero of the novel, however, is probably Marcus, the priest's brother, since he exhibits the greatest degree of moral progress.

21. See "The Idea of Perfection" in *The Sovereignty of Good;* and Peter Wolfe, *The Disciplined Heart: Iris Murdoch and Her Novels* (Columbia, Missouri: University of Missouri Press, 1966), chapter 9.

22. In Gnosticism and Neoplatonism, there was said to be in us a Divine element which was nonmaterial. This spark of the Divine was kept from returning to the Divine, from which it had become separated, by matter, which includes the human body. Hence both the body and the physical universe are to be shunned, regretted, and despised. What we are to respect, honor, and love would be the presence of the Divine in each one, not the full-particular, warts and all, that stands before us.

23. It is my impression that Murdoch herself does not believe that Plato sacrifices the particular to the general. See *The Sovereignty of Good*, pp. 93–97. See, however, Irving Singer, *The Nature of Love: Plato to Luther* (New York: Random House, 1966), pp. 21, 51–59, 72, 87–88.

CHAPTER THREE

1. There is serious controversy about the Biblical basis of this doctrine. Only Eichrodt of the major commentators believes it is present in Genesis 1. Others regard creation in Genesis 1 and 2 as the ordering of a preexistent chaos and the sustenance of order. But it is my view that the *ex nihilo* doctrine is sound theologically largely because of its relation, as we will see shortly, to the view of love with which we are concerned.

See Walther Eichrodt, "In the Beginning," in *Israel's Prophetic Heritage*, ed. Bernhard W. Anderson and Walter Harrelson (New York: Harper & Brothers, 1962), pp. 1–10. Anderson in his *Creation Versus Chaos* (New York: Association Press, 1967), pp. 111–12, supports Eichrodt.

2. All this is put temporally, and I think defensibly on a view in which time is created with the universe, as Augustine argues in his *Confessions*. But it is consistent to say that perhaps there was no beginning, yet all realities always depend on God for their existence. Hence there would be no other realities than God if God did not freely will that there be other realities in addition to himself; and he legitimately could become the only reality.

3. He still retains the brute power or capacity to annihilate these realities; and he morally could do so. For he could recognize their reality, just as we can recognize the reality of what we eat, and legitimately allow their annihilation or annihilate them himself.

4. Whitehead himself does not have a creator, only one who orders material. Some Process Theologians have a creator but retain the notion of a limited God. For though God is said to be perfect in his "primordial nature," the primordial nature of God is an abstraction, not a state or a condition such that God *could* remain alone.

5. A major reason for the denial of completeness by Process Theologians is that completeness has often been conceived in theology in Neoplatonic and Aristotelian terms. All action is motivated by a desire for the good, so that were one to act, it must be because one lacks something. Hence God, if complete, must not act; and if complete, he cannot be acted upon. They rightly insist that the Biblical God does act and is acted upon and hence Neoplatonism is an unsound philosophical model for a Christian doctrine of God. But one does not have to turn to a limited God in order to have a god who acts and who is acted upon. One can instead deny the theory of motivation that all action has a lack as its source, and thus have a complete God who acts.

6. Another difficult problem connected with the Christian doctrine of creation is to specify how God can be the source of all things *ex*

nihilo and yet leave room for men to have free will and responsibility. See Austin Farrer, *Faith and Speculation* (New York: New York University Press, 1967), chapters 4 and 5.

That the Christian doctrine of creation is riddled with problems should not be in itself surprising. A look at philosophical writing on the existence of the external world or other minds would reveal a mass of unresolved difficulties, even though we normally would not even dream of doubting that there are other minds and an external world.

7. It seems that the *ex nihilo* idea is a limiting idea or limiting case. We can conceive of it ontologically only as the progressive removal of material in instances of making: furniture made of wood (consisting of it); novelty emerging from material but not present in it before; a making by an agent by mere imagination. Yet we do not know by means of analogy whether there is anything that answers to the phrase "creation *ex nihilo.*" But something of what the doctrine of creation *ex nihilo* says has been presented concretely and conceivably with the view of love with which we are working.

8. *Orthodoxy* (New York: John Lane Company, 1908), pp. 107–8.

9. Process Theologians, in contrast to Aristotelian and Neoplatonic views which have been incorporated into the Christian doctrine of God, rightly stress that God is affected by us. But their alternative of a limited God does not permit the two acts of humility or love we have described, whereby God *becomes* dependent.

Moreover, their doctrine of the "consequent nature" of God, which is intended to allow for us to have an effect on him, does not itself affirm the consummation of love. In their terminology, our subjective reality (our consciousness) ceases at death. We have, however, "objective immortality" in that we are remembered and treasured by God; and, since we become or participate in his consequent nature by being so present to his awareness, we through him forever affect the universe. But this is not the doctrine of a God who loves us in such a way that he not only needs us and is affected by us but gives us *subjective* satisfaction as well. The Biblical view of love, which they rightly desire to articulate, requires a consummation of love: an indwelling whereby we give *and* receive.

10. The love of persons and things for their own sakes has not always been stressed in Christianity. Instead, Augustine's view that we are to find fulfillment in God alone, that is, that we are to love only him and to love others only through him, has had a deep and pervasive influence in Christianity. (See Irving Singer, *The Nature of Love: Plato to Luther* [New York: Random House, 1966].) But such a doctrine denies an essential element in love: the recognition of the reality of particulars.

11. This is also of course the same process by which many people learn to become more efficient at getting their own way.

CHAPTER FOUR

1. *Orthodoxy* (New York: John Lane Company, 1908), p. 243.

2. One wonders whether the Gospels are written from this standpoint. What they tell us about Jesus is not what scientific historical scholarship seeks in its search for a historical Jesus (Jesus as he "really" was without theological trappings). They tell us about Jesus' perception of us and what those who are able to see him as a particular see as their effect on him.

3. God the Father is more than this, and so too is the Son, but this is enough for Jesus Christ to be the divine Son.

4. This view is fully presented and defended in my book *The Reasonableness of Faith* (New York: World Publishing Company, 1968), esp. chapter 5.

CHAPTER FIVE

1. See Iris Murdoch, *The Sovereignty of Good* (New York: Schocken Books, Inc., 1971), pp. 87, 92.

2. Many of them are reviewed by James Norvell Lapsley in *Theology Today* (April, 1970).

In 1970 the journal *Omega*, dealing exclusively with the subject of death and related behavior, was launched.

3. *Presbyterian Life* (January 1, 1971), p. 7.

4. *Presbyterian Life* (September 15, 1970), p. 6.

5. See Lapsley, p. 91.

6. Wolfgang Stegmüller, *Main Currents in Contemporary German, British, and American Philosophy* (Bloomington, Indiana: Indiana University Press, 1970), p. 220. Stegmüller is here reporting the opinion of Nicolai Hartmann.

7. "Observations Regarding Death and Contemporary Secular and Theological Thought," an unpublished research paper.

8. So it may be that an individual's view of death or that of a society is such that the life after death promised by Christianity does not meet or resolve problems with death. An individual or a society may need to have the view of death modified before the Christian promise of life touches on anything which they need or which attracts them. On the other hand, Christianity may need to reshape its view of death, since it may legitimately need to blend with the distinctive ingredients of a particular social order.

9. Interestingly enough, though not addressed to the problem of an individual in an industrial society who must face his death as a socially

insignificant object, the notion of death as a blessing is commensurate at some points with what Talcott Parsons considers a rational and socially efficient view of death in an industrial society. He considers an orientation toward death as natural and good to be part of an ideal stance (once premature and painful death in a society have been greatly reduced by modern medicine). See his "Death in American Society—A Brief Working Paper," *American Behavioral Scientist* (May, 1963), pp. 61–65. This was pointed out to me by R. L. Staples.

10. Obviously this condition can be neurotic or pathological, but it also is equally obvious that it can be normal.

11. I have extended the Eastern churches' teaching that our suffering in purgatory (should there be one) is a purgation, not a punishment, because Christ pays for our sins.

12. In fact, suffering as a punishment is a major theme in the Old Testament, and in Christianity of the present day. I believe that I have given good grounds for rejecting this view, but to give a full case one would need to undertake the prodigious task of arguing Biblically and from the history of doctrine that it is incorrect to believe that God punishes.

13. It will not necessarily be received by all people, not because God will withhold it from some as a punishment but because it is *our* task to move from our *de facto* position to a recognition of the reality of others, including God's reality. He respects us as realities: it is our task to overcome the illusion of our *de facto* selves, an illusion based in part on our very reality (on our actual worth).

14. Our mutual indwelling with each other and him is a complication which has been left out here, but it was carefully affirmed in our treatment of the kingdom of God.

Chapter Six

1. The soundness of this assumption and its relevance to our argument here is examined in my article "Resurrection Appearances as Evidence," *Theology Today* (April, 1973).

2. That the response of faith is a sufficient ground to affirm and adhere to the truth of the gospel is argued in detail in my book *The Reasonableness of Faith.*

Chapter Seven

1. As found in W. E. H. Lecky, *History of the Rise and Influence of the Spirit of Rationalism in Europe,* rev. ed. (New York: D. Appleton and Company, 1872), Vol. I, p. 183.

2. "A Discourse of Miracles," *The Reasonableness of Christianity with "A Discourse of Miracles" and part of "A Third Letter Concern-*

ing Toleration," ed. I. T. Ramsey (Stanford, California: Stanford University Press, 1958), p. 82.

3. *The Need for Roots,* trans. Arthur Wills (New York: G. P. Putnam's Sons, 1952), p. 268.

4. "God and the Rural Poor," *Psychology Today* (January, 1972), pp. 31–41.